General Principles of
Business and Economic Law

General Principles of
Business and Economic Law

An Introduction to Contemporary Legal
Principles Governing Private and Public
Economic Activity at the National and
Supranational Levels

John W. Head
UNIVERSITY OF KANSAS SCHOOL OF LAW

CAROLINA ACADEMIC PRESS

Durham, North Carolina

MT

ISBN: 978-1-59460-419-5
LCCN: 2007936557

Carolina Academic Press
700 Kent Street
Durham, North Carolina 27701
Telephone (919) 489-7486
Fax (919) 493-5668
www.cap-press.com

Printed in the United States of America.

2/3/10

Summary Contents

Detailed Table of Contents

Preface & Acknowledgments

Anyone who benefits from this book owes a lot to Cliff Thompson. Professor Thompson, who has served as the dean of numerous law schools both in the USA and elsewhere, is a colleague and friend of mine who directed a long-term, highly successful legal education project in Indonesia that started in the mid-1990s and lasted about a decade. It was in helping some with that project—the so-called "ELIPS" Project*—that I proposed to prepare a short book on "economic law". Professor Thompson embraced that idea and made sure that the book—titled A General Introduction to Economic Law— got printed, distributed, and used widely in Indonesia.

Even after the conclusion of the ELIPS project a few years ago, Professor Thompson has continued his support for legal education in Indonesia. One form that his continued support has taken is the publication of revised editions of the earlier General Introduction book and some other ELIPS-generated books for use in Indonesia. Moreover, seeing the benefit that such efforts have brought to that country, Professor Thompson has encouraged me to prepare a new version of the General Introduction book for audiences outside Indonesia.

Hence this book. As explained more fully in my remarks under "The Aim, Perspective, and Structure of this Book", I hope that having this revised work published by Carolina Academic Press will prove beneficial to a broad audience in several countries—including not

---

* The ELIPS Project, financed in part by the US Agency for International Development, first focused on "Economic Law and Improved Procurement Systems" and later concentrated on "Economic Law, Institutional and Professional Strengthening".

only the USA but also several other countries in which there is a serious need to develop the legal infrastructure, and particularly the programs of legal education, that are so necessary in order to prosper in a globalized economy.

In the way of thanks and acknowledgments, therefore, I would give particular attention to the work of the ELIPS Project and its dedicated staff, to the University of Indonesia (where much of the ELIPS work was headquartered and which assisted in the printing and distribution of numerous books emerging from the ELIPS Project), and to the University of Wisconsin, which served as the institutional home for further printing and distribution efforts. My own work has been personally aided greatly by the contributions of numerous other people, including Adijayah Yusuf, Irene Sulaiman, Putti Ranni Damai, and other Indonesian friends and colleagues—and of course by my colleagues at the University of Kansas Law School. Particularly helpful contributions of time and guidance came from Professors Phil DeLaTorre, Chris Drahozal, Webb Hecker, and Stephen Ware, as well as from Lucia Orth. Research assistance was given generously, cheerfully, and patiently by Alexandra Lasley English, Katie Lula, and Christine Ohlen, to whom I give special thanks. Support from the University of Kansas General Research Fund is also, as always, gratefully acknowledged.

List of Acronyms

CIF	cost, insurance, and freight
CISG	United Nations Convention on Contracts for the International Sale of Goods
CoCom	the Coordinating Committee on Multilateral Export Controls
ECOSOC	Economic and Social Council (of the United Nations)
EU	European Union
FIFO	first in, first out
FOB	free on board
GATT	General Agreement on Tariffs and Trade
G-7	Group of Seven (USA, UK, France, Germany, Japan, Italy, and Canada)
G-8	the Group of Seven plus the Russian Republic
GUIDEC	General Usage for International Digitally Ensured Commerce
ICANN	the Internet Corporation for Assigned Names and Numbers
ICC	International Chamber of Commerce
ICSID	International Centre for the Settlement of Investment Disputes
ILO	International Labour Organization
IMF	International Monetary Fund

INCOTERMS	international commercial terms, issued by the ICC
ITO	International Trade Organization (never created)
LIFO	last in, first out
MIGA	Multilateral Investment Guarantee Agency
MFN	most-favored nation
NTB	non-tariff barrier
OECD	Organisation for Economic Cooperation and Development
REACH	the EU's Registration, Evaluation, and Authorization of Chemicals program
TRIMs	[Agreement on] Trade-Related Investment Measures
TRIPs	[Agreement on] Trade-Related Aspects of Intellectual Property Rights
UCP	Uniform Customs and Practice, issued by the ICC
ULB	Uniform Law on Bills of Exchange and Promissory Notes
UNCITRAL	United Nations Commission on International Trade Law
UNDP	United Nations Development Program
VAT	value-added tax
WIPO	World Intellectual Property Organization
WTO	World Trade Organization

Introduction

The Aim, Perspective, and Structure of This Book

About the Term "Economic Law"

This book is designed to give readers a basic familiarity with several key topics that they should know about in order to understand the relationship between law and economic activity. Any country's economic development—and, on an individual level, the economic well-being of a particular individual or family or business entity—takes place within the context of laws. Some of those laws provide the means by which individuals can join together into companies for the purpose of carrying out business. Some establish a system by which that business can get access to banking services, such as financing for the purchase and sale of goods. Other laws set forth minimum requirements as to how a company should treat its employees, or refrain from damaging the environment, or conduct its business fairly.

This complicated web of law is often referred to as "economic law" or as "business law". In my view, the first of these two terms ("economic law") is the more accurate and descriptive of the two because it casts a "wider net" of meaning—and, as will become clear from the pages that follow, the relationship between law and economic activity encompasses a great many subjects indeed. The term "business law", however, is more familiar in some countries, including for example, the USA, and it is in deference to this familiarity of usage that I have settled on the title for this book: General Principles of Business and Economic Law.

The Intended Audience for This Book

Despite the great breadth of coverage that the term "business and economic law" entails, this book is in fact quite short and can only offer a very brief account of business and economic law. But it is short for a particular purpose. The aim is to provide a condensed overview—a synopsis—of economic law that is straightforward enough to be understood by non-experts. By "non-experts" I mean particularly students falling in two categories. The first category comprises those students who are entering into a study of law, whether at the undergraduate or graduate level, and who wish to undertake an introductory study of "economic law" as I have defined it above. Such law students might be enrolled in a course titled "Business Law", or they might be taking an even more general introductory course that includes one unit focusing on the subjects covered in this book.

Without doubt, law students who are concentrating their studies in business and economic law will proceed to take further, more detailed courses in several of the topics summarized in this book. For them, this book can serve as a foundation for those more detailed studies. On the other hand, for students who are not concentrating their studies in business and economic law, this book (and the course in which it is assigned as reading) can provide an overall introduction to an important area of law, with which all lawyers should have some familiarity.

The other category of students for whom this book is designed comprises those who are not focusing their studies on law at all but who are instead concentrating on political science or economics or business or a wide range of other disciplines that involve issues lying at the intersection of economic activity, political governance, and social organization. This book can help those students understand what a central role law plays in dealing with such issues. That role of law is important to understand, because law is society's official method of imposing requirements, establishing procedures, offering solutions, resolving disputes, and reflecting societal values.

This book is designed also for an audience other than students. Law in general—and economic law in particular—increasingly affects the lives of everyone in society, including those involved in business, banking, employment, accounting, construction, manufacturing, or the arts. The condensed overview of economic law provided in the following pages can also, I hope, be of interest and assistance to them.

Focusing on "General Principles"

Most law is *national* law. That is, the rules that govern behavior, including economic activity, exist at the level of a particular country. Only a relatively few such rules are international in scope or source. This fact reflects the current importance of the nation-state in today's world. There are just under 200 nation-states in the world, and most of the laws in each are different from those in all the rest. Therefore, the practicing lawyer must look mainly to his or her own country for the specific legal rules that apply in a particular case.

Despite this diversity in specific legal rules, certain basic concepts do hold true in most countries. That is, some general principles of law are global in applicability and underlie the specific rules in most countries. It is those general principles, specifically in the area of business and economic law, that this book tries to identify and explain. In addition, the book also discusses some rules that have been explicitly agreed to at the international level; these include rules on international business transactions and international economic relations. Reflecting the increasing importance of those topics, they are dealt with in slightly more detail here than are the other topics of economic law.

In order to determine how best to structure a particular transaction, or how much tax to pay on business profits, or how to handle similar detailed matters, the applicable rules of the local and national jurisdiction must be studied and applied. This book is not intended to provide any answers to those specific questions. Instead, it aims to build a broad foundation of knowledge on which the applicable laws can be more intelligently understood and applied. In most cases, of course, trained lawyers should be employed to advise on specific issues, and therefore the faculties at law schools and universities will be responsible for building on the foundation described in this book, by providing instruction in the specific rules.

Structure of This Book

The structure of the book reflects my own views about the conceptual organization of the rules of business and economic law. Many different formulations, of course, would be possible. If this book is used in the context of a specific university or law school course, the instructor might assign readings in whatever order he or she chooses. In general, however, the book tries to follow a logical path, and some of the later chapters build on discussions appearing in earlier chapters.

The book has four chapters. Chapter I explores the role and operations of business entities in the economy and covers topics of business organizations, competition law (to guard against monopolies and other perceived evils), business financing techniques, accounting rules, and bankruptcy. Chapter II covers some especially important transactional aspects of business operations: commercial transactions, settlement of disputes arising out of such transactions, banking and insurance law and practice, intellectual property protection, and cyber law. Chapter III turns to government regulation, particularly in the areas of labor law, natural resources, consumer protection, and taxation. Chapter IV examines international commerce and investment and the key international institutions that regulate such activity.

Within each chapter, related areas of law are discussed in general terms. Following each discussion is a list of further reading materials that might be of interest to learn more about the subject just discussed.

Technical Matters and Conventions

In this book I have followed certain conventions on punctuation and usage that might be unfamiliar to some readers. These conventions include the following:

- I have followed the less-used but more logical convention of placing quotation marks inside all punctuation (unless of course the punctuation itself is included in the original material being quoted). Doing so allows the text to reflect more faithfully how the original material reads.

- The possessive form of words that end in the letter "s" have not had another letter "s" added to them—hence "the business' assets", not "the business's assets".
- The acronym noun "USA" is often used in this book in preference to the longer noun "United States", inasmuch as there are other countries (such as Mexico) with the title "United States" in their official names. However, the term "US" has been retained for use as an adjective referring to something of or from the United States, such as "US legislation" or "US states".[1]

Although this book is short, it is designed to provide access to further detail by offering citations to authorities and additional reading. I have used footnotes to cite the books, articles, treaties, and other legal materials that serve as authority for quoted or attributed passages in the main text. Those citations appear in a less abbreviated style than that used by US law journals and many US law books. I believe the heavily abbreviated style used in US legal texts can be so unfamiliar to a student audience (and obviously to a more general audience) as to create confusion or uncertainty. In addition, in the case of books, I have departed from the practice of putting the authors' names in all capital letters. Instead, authors' names for all works—books and articles and other items—appear in regular upper case and lower case letters; then titles of books appear in large and small capitals and titles of other works appear in italics or, in a few cases depending on the nature of the work, in regular font with quotation marks. An even more simplified form of citation is used in the "Further Readings" entries appearing at the end of each substantive discussion.

---

1. In this book I have opted for the use of "US" and "USA" without periods, as this seems to be the more modern trend and also follows the usage found in acronyms for other political entities such as the United Nations (UN) and the People's Republic of China (PRC). Naturally, I have not changed "U.S." to "US" in any quoted material or official citations.

General Principles of
Business and Economic Law

Chapter I

The Role of Business Entities in the Economy

A large proportion of economic activity at all levels (international, national, and local) involves business entities. These business entities may be involved in the manufacturing of goods, the sale of goods, the transport of goods, the provision of services, the hiring of employees, and countless other activities that affect everyone in society.

Hence it makes sense for us to focus first on legal rules that bear directly on how such business entities are structured, what their attributes are, how they get the financial resources they need to carry out their operations, what measures they need to take in order to account for those financial resources, and how they are to be treated when they enter into serious financial difficulties. This chapter addresses all of those topics and a few others.

I.A. Business Organizations

This introduction to business and economic law begins with an overview of business organizations because it is through these organizations, these legal associations of persons, that all economic activity takes place. Business organizations are the vehicles of economic activity. They are the entities that are concerned with and governed by most of the rules and procedures described in this book—including competition rules, business financing, accounting, and bankruptcy (sections B through E of this Chapter), as well as commercial contracts, secured lending, labor law, product liability, and international sales of goods (see Chapters II through IV).

The organization of business is a matter of national law. Various countries have developed a wide range of business forms—that is, types of business organizations. As noted above in the "Aim, Perspective, and Structure" comments, this book does not attempt to explain the details of any particular country's law. Instead, it offers a general view of several key topics within the area of economic law. Hence, the following paragraphs identify the more important varieties of business organizations found in a great many national legal systems. In short, the aim is to provide a broad exposure to the possible forms of business organization and, perhaps most importantly, to the central features or purposes that these various forms of business organization reveal.

In distinguishing between diverse types of business organization, four issues or questions[1] should be borne in mind:

- Creation ... how is it formed?
- Liability ... when can third parties sue the owners?
- Duties ... what do the participants owe each other?
- Termination ... when does it end?

These questions yield different answers for each of the principal forms of business organization identified below. Those forms are: sole proprietorship, partnership, limited partnership, limited liability company, stock company (called public corporation in most common law countries), and cooperative. Also discussed below are government enterprises and multinational enterprises.

I.A.1. Sole Proprietorship; Partnership; Limited Partnership

A *sole proprietorship*, or single-owner business, is the simplest type of business entity to organize and to operate. It has been described in

---

1. These four points appear in George D. Cameron III, The Legal and Regulatory Environment of Business (South-Western Publishing, 1994), at page 267. The following paragraphs draw substantially from this source, as well as from chapter 4 of Ray August, International Business Law (Prentice Hall, 1993) [hereinafter cited as August-1993]. Updated information in this regard is available in Ray August, International Business Law (3d edition, 2000) [hereinafter cited as August-2000].

this way: "One person has all management authority, so decisions can be reached quickly. That feature may be a plus or a minus, depending on the ability of the sole owner. It may also be more difficult to raise capital, since only one person is responsible for the debts of the business."[2] Indeed, it is this practical limitation that has led to the creation of business organizations involving more than one person.

Because only one person is involved in a sole proprietorship, the other issues raised above are easy to address. First, there is no separate creation process because there is no separate "business" as such. There might, however, be registration requirements, as the government authorities responsible for regulating business activities will need to know what businesses are subject to regulation—such as the rules on taxation, health and safety, insurance, and the like. Second, the owner of a sole proprietorship has full, unlimited personal liability for all debts and liabilities of the business. Thus, a failure of the business can lead to the loss not only of the business assets but the personal assets of the owner. Third, there are no duties among owners because there is only one owner. Lastly, termination of a sole proprietorship takes place when the sole owner decides to terminate it, or when it is terminated by reason of bankruptcy or the death of the owner.

A *partnership* is a combination of two or more persons organized to carry on a business as co-owners and co-managers. (Here, as in the other forms of business organization, it is assumed that the purpose of the business is to make a profit; this distinguishes business organizations from groups formed for charitable, social, or other non-business purposes.) In most cases, each member of a partnership is personally liable for the entire obligations of the partnership.

As for the four issues identified above: (1) a partnership can usually be created with little or no formality, and typically with no government approval being required, although registration with the appropriate government agency or agencies will almost always be necessary; (2) as noted above, each partner is fully liable for the obligations of the partnership, subject to certain exceptions that some countries provide for (the largest exception being, in fact, the limited partnership arrange-

---

2. Cameron, *supra* note 1, at page 274.

ments discussed below); (3) because so much is at stake for each partner, the relevant law usually demands that each partner fulfill duties of fair dealing, honesty, and fiduciary responsibility toward the other partners, and that no partner can make personal use of the business property without the consent of all other partners; (4) termination is triggered by several circumstances, including (i) the bankruptcy of the business, (ii) a voluntary winding-up of the partnership's operations, and usually (iii) a change in the number or identity of the partners, unless a partnership agreement establishes a method for determining how to pay off a departing partner (or the estate of a deceased partner) and how much to charge an incoming new partner.

A *limited partnership* is designed to overcome one of the major disadvantages of a partnership—the unlimited personal liability of each partner for the obligations of the business. The limited partnership form of business organization does this by permitting some of the owner-partners to enjoy limited personal liability as long as they comply with all legal requirements. It is this feature that characterizes the limited partnership and makes it attractive.

As an example, assume that one person, Mr. Erman, wants to open a grocery business but does not have enough capital of his own to do so. He might ask two or three other people to join him in a limited partnership, under an arrangement by which (i) those other people would provide the beginning capital, (ii) Mr. Erman would run the business, and (iii) they would all split the profits (or losses) equally among them. Once such a limited partnership is created (it might require government approval), Mr. Erman would be the "general partner" and would have unlimited liability; the "limited partners" would have liability only to the extent of their contribution of capital.

The duties among partners in a limited partnership vary depending on the status of the partner involved. A general partner owes the same duties of honesty and competence as in a regular partnership. Limited partners typically are not involved in the management of the business—in fact, they risk losing their limitation of liability if they do participate in the management—and their duties are correspondingly less.

In general, a limited partnership is more durable than a regular partnership. That is, the number and identity of the limited partners can change rather easily without affecting the continuity of the business organization itself. Indeed, it is the fact of limited liability and ease of entry and exit that makes a limited partnership an attractive way of investing in a business and therefore an important method of financing a business undertaking.

In some countries (including the USA) yet another type of partnership has been established: the *limited liability partnership*. Typically such a business organization is almost identical to the general partnership for of business organization, except that all partners have limited liability.

I.A.2. Limited Liability Company; Stock Company; Cooperative

The term *limited liability company* is subject to various meanings. In most civil law systems (that is, legal systems sharing the civil law tradition, which has its roots in Roman law and which was spread throughout Europe and later throughout much of the rest of the world), a limited liability company is a separate legal entity whose ownership interests (held by persons sometimes called "associates") are not traded publicly, and whose financial statements do not need to be disclosed to the public.[3] The term "limited liability company" carries a different meaning in most common law systems (that is, legal systems growing out of the English common law tradition, such as the USA and Australia);[4] in those systems a different type of entity, the "close corporation", resembles the civil-law limited liability company. Literature and laws on business organizations can be confusing because of these divergent definitions.

The four issues identified above—creation, liability, duties, and termination—apply as follows in the case of a typical (civil law) limited liability company. First, it is created by means of a series of steps that usually include: (i) the preparation and submission of a set of ar-

---

3. August-1993, *supra* note 1, at page 150.

4. Cameron, *supra* note 1, at page 287. In some states of the USA, a "limited liability company" is essentially partnership with limited liability, in which all members can participate in management without losing their limited liability. *Id.*

ticles of association (or articles of incorporation) that identify the company's name, the location of its office, its purpose, and the capital invested; (ii) the pledging of the required minimum amount of capital; and (iii) the issuance of an approval by the responsible government agency and public notification of that fact. Second, the successful creation of a such an entity results in limited liability for all participants. Indeed, that is both the appeal of the limited liability company and the reason that formalities and legal requirements have to be followed very carefully in its creation. A member of the public making a claim against the company is generally not permitted to claim against the personal assets of its owners, except in cases (i) where defects occurred in establishing the company or (ii) where other unusual or illegal circumstances make it necessary to "pierce the corporate veil"—that is, to look beyond the "walls" of the company—and impose personal liability on the owners.

It is worth pointing out, however, that the liability of the company itself is not limited. As one author has noted, "[t]he liability of the company to pay its debts is *unlimited* in the sense that it must pay all debts due from it so long as its assets are sufficient to meet them."[5] In short, it is the individual owners of the company, not the company itself, as to which liability is limited.

Third, the principal duties among the persons involved in a limited liability company typically fall on the officers and directors—that is, on the persons responsible for the management of the company. They owe to the company and its owners a fiduciary duty (an especially demanding legal duty to handle the affairs of the company with care and for the benefit of the company and its owners, rather than for their own personal benefit). The functions of the owners include electing the company's directors, enacting the bylaws or other internal rules of procedure, approving annual reports on operations, and declaring dividends (amounts to be paid proportionally to the owners out of the company's annual profits). However, the paying of such dividends, as well as many other financial actions taken by the company and its

---

5. Kenneth Smith and Denis Keenan, COMPANY LAW (Pitman Publishing, 5th ed., 1983), at page 7 (emphasis added).

managers and owners, is usually subject to legal restrictions designed to guard against an impairment of the company's capital.

Because the ownership interests in a limited liability company are not publicly traded, the transfer of those ownership rights can sometimes be difficult and subject to restrictions. As for the issue of termination: limited liability companies typically have perpetual existence but can be wound up voluntarily or in case of bankruptcy.

A *stock company*, like a limited liability company, constitutes a separate legal entity in which each owner's liability is limited to the amount of his or her ownership interest. Typically, the distinguishing marks of a stock company are (i) the fact that its shares are freely traded among the public and (ii) the requirement that its financial statements be disclosed to the public. The corresponding form of business organization in many common law countries is the *public corporation*.

Of all the various forms of business organization, the stock company (and its common law relative, the publicly-traded corporation) has drawn the most attention in recent years because of its growing importance in the economic life of many countries. With the combination of (a) limitation on liability and (b) ease of movement in and out of ownership, this form of business organization has been called the "steam engine" of capitalism.[6] It permits the accumulation of individual savings for a common business purpose in an amount greater than almost any single person could dream of, but at the same time allows any individual investor the freedom of removing his or her ownership interest at will.

Many of the attributes of a stock company are similar to those of a limited liability company as described above. Typically, a stock company is created when the responsible government agency approves the

---

6. See Richard M. Buxbaum, *A Comparative View of Modern Company Law* (presentation for ELIPS seminar in Indonesia in August 1994; on file with author), at page 1. The same authority has used the term "marketable share companies" as a general label for "stock" or "public" companies of the type described here—that is, companies whose shares are publicly traded. Richard M. Buxbaum, *The Formation of Marketable Share Companies*, in INTERNATIONAL ENCYCLOPEDIA OF COMPARATIVE LAW (Vol. XIII, Ch. 3), at pages 1–2 (Oceana Publications, 1972).

company's proposed articles of incorporation, the requirements of which are prescribed in the applicable company laws. Each person having an ownership interest in the company carries liability limited to the amount of that person's investment. The officers and directors owe important fiduciary duties to the company and its shareholders.[7] The company normally has perpetual existence, subject of course to voluntary winding-up or liquidation through bankruptcy proceedings. Termination of a stock company can also come by way of its merger into or with another stock company.[8]

A key difference between the stock company and the limited liability company is its public nature. Partly because its shares are traded publicly, the stock company has heavy responsibilities of fair disclosure (to the public) of its financial condition and operations. Indeed, many of the rules of accounting described in section D of this Chapter arise from the public nature of stock companies: potential investors require accurate and understandable financial information about the company before they will be willing to invest in it. Sometimes the size of a stock company (particularly the overall value of its assets) will bear on the level of detail that it is required to provide in its financial statements; indeed, the regulatory requirements applicable to large stock companies are often more extensive in several respects than those applicable to smaller stock companies.

Another form of business organization that shares some features of limited liability companies and stock companies is the *cooperative*. The details regarding this type of entity vary greatly from one legal system to another; and indeed, this form of business organization is used extensively in some countries but is used very little in others. In the USA, for example, cooperatives are used mainly in the food and

---

7. For an old survey of various national laws governing these issues, see Bernhard Grossfeld, *Management and Control of Marketable Share Companies*, in INTERNATIONAL ENCYCLOPEDIA OF COMPARATIVE LAW (Vol. XIII, Ch. 4) (Oceana Publications, 1973).

8. For a survey of various national laws relating to termination (including merger) of stock companies, see Alfred Conard, *Fundamental Changes in Marketable Share Companies*, in INTERNATIONAL ENCYCLOPEDIA OF COMPARATIVE LAW (Vol. XIII, Ch. 6) (Oceana Publications, 1972).

agriculture industries; they are not used so much in other segments of the economy.

In general, a cooperative is a business that is owned and democratically controlled by the people who use its services and whose benefits are derived and distributed equitably on the basis of use. The user-owners, often called members, benefit in two ways from the cooperative, in proportion to the use they make of it. First, the more they use the cooperative, the more service they receive. Second, earnings from the cooperative are allocated to members based on the amount of business they do with the cooperative. Details in these respects, and the presence or absence of others features of cooperatives, depend on specific national laws.

I.A.3. Government Enterprises

A *government enterprise* is one that is owned mainly or exclusively by the state. Such entities appear in most legal systems, although their number and influence vary greatly from one country to another. Their operations can be in the areas of finance, trade, industry, agriculture, mining, health, transportation, and other sectors of the economy, including electric, water, and sanitation services. In some cases they are designed to maximize profits, but in most cases their dominant aim is public service—that is, benefitting the country as a whole.

The methods of creating such government enterprises vary widely, but typically the most important such enterprises are specifically established by legislation. Such legislation will serve as the charter of the enterprise, indicating its aims, financial status, methods of operations, management, and so forth. Accompanying such legislation will be legislative or executive action to provide the funding for capitalizing and operating the enterprise.[9]

An example of a government enterprise is a country's central bank. In most countries, the central bank is established as a separate legal

---

9. For a survey of various national laws relating to government enterprises, see Wolfgang Friedmann, *Governmental (Public) Enterprises*, in INTERNATIONAL ENCYCLOPEDIA OF COMPARATIVE LAW (Vol. XIII, Ch. 13) (Oceana Publications, 1972).

entity, with a degree of financial and operational independence from the short-term political pressures of government. Ultimate accountability of the central bank (or similar government enterprise) to the state is assured in large part (i) by providing for government appointment of top managers or directors and (ii) by enumerating in the chartering legislation the specific array of powers and functions granted to the central bank (or similar government enterprise). (For further details on central banks, see section C of Chapter II, below.)

I.A.4. Multinational Enterprises

An increasing number of business entities carry out operations internationally. Although most such operations are discussed in Chapter IV of this book, the role of such business entities—often referred to as *multinational enterprises*—warrants a brief discussion here of their structure.

One source provides the following set of definitions[10] generally used in international practice to describe various structures and relationships within multinational enterprises:

national multinational enterprise	an enterprise organized around a parent firm incorporated in one country that operates through branches and subsidiaries in other countries.
international multinational enterprise	an enterprise that operates through branches and subsidiaries and that has parent companies in two or more countries.
parent company	a company that acts as the head office for a multi-national enterprise and which owns and controls the enterprise's subsidiary entities.
branch	a unit or part of a company, not separately incorporated.

---

10. August-1993, *supra* note 1, at page 159.

agent	an independent person or company with authority to act on behalf of the enterprise.
representative office	an office that interested parties can contact to obtain information about the company but that is not empowered to conduct business for the company.
holding company	a company owned by a parent company to supervise and coordinate the operations of subsidiary companies.
subsidiary	a company that is owned by a parent or a parent's holding company but which, unlike a branch, is separately incorporated as a legal entity.
joint venture	an association of persons or companies collaborating in a business venture for more than a short or transitory time period.

These various types of entities are subject, of course, to regulation by any state in whose territory they operate. To a very limited extent, multinational enterprises are also subject to a few guidelines of conduct issued by international bodies, but these are mainly non-binding in character.

Further Readings on Business Organizations
(in addition to the sources cited in the footnotes in this section)

International Encyclopedia of Laws: Corporations and Partnerships (1996), edited by Koen Geens

Hornbook on the Law of Agency and Partnership (1990), by Harold Gill Reuschlein; *The Law of Agency and Partnership* (Third Edition, 2001), by Harold Gill Reuschlein and William A. Gregory

Corporations and Other Business Associations: Statutes, Rules and Forms (2000 edition), selected and edited by Edward S. Adams and John H. Matheson

European Corporate Law (1995), by Adriaan Dorresteijn

Corporate Law (Eleventh Edition, 1989), by Robert Charles Clark

The Law of Corporations in a Nutshell (Fifth Edition, 2000), by Robert W. Hamilton

Corporate Control and Accountability (1994), edited by Joseph McCahery, Sol Picciotto, and Colin Scott

Companies and Other Legal Persons under Netherlands Law (updated to 1996), edited by H. C. S. Warendorf and R. L. Thomas

Company Law (Fifth Edition, 1983), by Kenneth Smith and Denis Keenan

Foundations of Corporate Law (1993), edited by Roberta Romano

Company Law—Nutshell (Fourth Edition, 2001), by F. Rose

I.B. Competition Law

I.B.1. The Goal of Promoting Competition

The term "competition law" refers to laws and regulations designed to ensure an adequate degree of competition among business entities operating in an economy. Perhaps more than any other topic of economic law, competition law reflects a particular economic ideology or philosophy. It is an economic philosophy that is now very widely accepted in the world (following the collapse of the Soviet Union, which was the main proponent of central economic planning). The philosophy has been expressed in this way:

> Many people argue that vigorous competition lowers the price of goods and promotes the efficient allocation of resources. Competition also limits business power; in a competitive market, individuals cannot take advantage of the people with whom they deal. If a seller charges too high a price for wares, buyers are able to purchase them from someone else. Many people regard this alternative as producing fairer results than would decisions by … the government as to what and how much to produce. Arguably competition

also helps to keep business small and opportunity open for everyone, and to distribute money throughout society rather than to a few powerful people.[11]

Put more simply, competition is considered a good thing because competition will require producers (of goods or services) to strive to satisfy customer desires at the lowest price with the use of the fewest resources. Hence the key aim of competition law is to promote competition.

The precise method of achieving that aim of promoting competition varies, of course, from one national legal system to the next. Sometimes, a nation will adopt rules regarding competition via both national legislation and international conventions. For instance, all member states of the European Union have national competition laws that operate alongside the EU's overall competition laws. Member states that did not have their own national competition laws drafted new ones based upon the EU's laws, whereas member states that did already have their own national competition laws simply amended their laws to integrate the EU's laws.[12]

I.B.2. Behaviors that Competition Laws Regulate

The specific details of various national laws around the world in this regard are beyond the scope of this book, but certain general themes do emerge from those national laws. Here is a fairly comprehensive list of the types of behavior that competition laws might prohibit or restrict:

- monopolies
- market allocations
- price fixing
- resale price maintenance
- group boycotts

---

11. Douglas Whitman and John William Gergacz, THE LEGAL AND SOCIAL ENVIRONMENT OF BUSINESS (McGraw-Hill, 1994), at page 650.

12. See Lennart Ritter & W. David Braun, EUROPEAN COMPETITION LAW: A PRACTITIONER'S GUIDE (3d ed. 2004), at pages 14–15.

- tying arrangements
- mergers

A *monopoly* has been defined as "a business entity that deliberately engages in conduct to obtain or maintain the power to control prices or exclude competition in some part of trade or commerce."[13] A business entity that is the only one operating in a particular market is obviously a monopoly (or "has a monopoly" in that market). But even if there are several business entities in a particular market, one of them can still in fact have a monopoly if the other entities lack the power to influence overall prices or output in the market. In contrast to a monopoly, a competitive system includes many business entities each producing the same product or service, with none of the business entities individually possessing the power to control overall prices or output.

Determining whether or not a monopoly exists requires a definition of the relevant market. Usually a market is defined both in terms of geography and in terms of product. For example, assume the following hypothetical facts: (i) a business entity named Handle, Inc., located in Detroit, Michigan manufactures household-sized diesel-powered electrical generators and sells them throughout Canada and the USA; (ii) there are other manufacturers of electrical generators located in Canada, but none of them makes household-sized models; (iii) there are other manufacturers of household-sized generators in the USA, but only in the southeast part of the country, and the cost of transporting those products to Canada is prohibitively expensive. On these facts, it would appear that Handle, Inc. has a monopoly in the Canada market for household-sized diesel-powered electrical generators. It does not have a monopoly in terms of electrical generators in general, nor does it have a monopoly in any product in all of the USA. But it does have a monopoly in its own particular geographic and product market.

Although it might be argued that monopolies are not necessarily bad—after all, a concentration of resources in one business entity can lead to efficiencies of scale—the more widely accepted view is that monopolies are bad (with certain exceptions) because a company enjoying a monopoly can raise the prices of goods and services at will, without

---

13. Whitman & Gergacz, *supra* note 11, at page 671.

the discipline imposed by competition. Therefore, competition laws often give special scrutiny to monopolies, prohibiting them in most circumstances. They are not prohibited, however, in businesses that are considered "natural monopolies" (such as some utilities companies) or in cases where control over some type of property or operation serves other important purposes. For example, copyrights and patent rights permit persons to exercise monopoly rights over the production of certain types of products, but such monopolies are considered justified in order to encourage persons to be creative, by protecting (for a limited time) their right to use the fruits of their creativity.

In addition to monopolies, competition laws often prohibit or restrict various other types of conduct having the effect of placing restraints on competition. For example, an agreement among ten companies to create a *horizontal market division*—under which each company would only sell products in a particular specified territory—would often be prohibited by competition laws. In the EU, such horizontal agreements are prohibited—as are *vertical agreements*, which are arrangements under which a producer grants a distributor the exclusive right to distribute its products solely in a certain nation, region, or territory.[14] Likewise, a *price fixing* arrangement among several business entities, under which they all agreed not to charge less than a specified price for a particular product, would often be prohibited.

A *resale price maintenance* arrangement represents a special type of price fixing, in which a single manufacturer and a retail seller agree to set either the maximum price or the minimum price at which a commodity may be resold. The problem with such an arrangement, according to one source, is as follows:

> [I]t prevents competition between retailers. If a television manufacturer required all television sets be sold at no more than a certain price, every retailer would be forced to sell the televisions at a price somewhere between the wholesale price and the maximum price. This would lead, possibly, to very little competition at the retail level.[15]

---

14. See Ritter & Braun, *supra* note 12, at pages 69–70.
15. Whitman & Gergacz, *supra* note 11, at page 688.

If a business entity collaborates with another business entity to refuse to deal with a third business entity, this is called a *group boycott*. Some competition laws prohibit such behavior. A group boycott would exist, for example, if four manufacturers of chairs, desiring to eliminate competition from a Company X (another manufacturer of chairs) informed all of their customers—that is, the various small retail companies purchasing chairs from them—that if those retailers also purchased chairs from Company X, the first four manufacturers would stop selling chairs to those retailers.

Similar in concept to a group boycott is a *tying arrangement*, in which a seller asks a buyer to purchase certain goods from the seller in addition to those that the buyer really wants. For example, the business entity referred to above, Handle, Inc., might require a buyer, as a condition of purchasing one of Handle's electrical generators, to purchase also (i) a specified quantity of diesel fuel to run the generator and (ii) a specified quantity of electrical wiring used to connect the generator to a building's electrical supply. In some competition laws, such a tying arrangement is illegal.

Certain types of *mergers*—that is, legal combinations of formerly separate business entities—are also prohibited under most competition laws. By now the reasoning should be obvious: if a merger of two or more business entities into a single business entity is likely to have the purpose and effect of reducing competition (perhaps even creating a monopoly), then it should be disallowed. Mergers can take many forms. A horizontal merger involves a merger between two companies that formerly competed with each other in the same product and geographic market. A vertical merger involves a combination between a customer (or several customers) and a supplier. For example, if Handle, Inc., referred to above, purchased (and in that way merged with) all the other manufacturers of household-sized diesel-powered electrical generators in the USA, it would be a horizontal merger; if Handle, Inc. purchased all the retailers involved in selling such generators and the wiring used in installing them, it would be a vertical merger. Under some competition laws, both types of merger would be scrutinized by government agencies responsible for ensuring against anticompetitive behavior.

In placing prohibitions or restrictions on the various types of behavior described above, legal systems aim at promoting competition and forbidding businesses from getting into a position (or using that position in a way) that will work to the detriment of consumers. In some cases the legal prohibitions or restrictions are given far-reaching effect. For example, US "antitrust" laws have been given a large degree of extraterritorial application (that is, application outside the territory of the USA), often triggering harsh criticism by companies and other governments.

Further Readings on Competition Law

(in addition to the sources cited in the footnotes in this section)

International Antitrust Law & Policy 1994 (1995), edited by Barry E. Hawk

International Antitrust Law & Policy—Annual Proceedings of the Fordham Corporate Law Institute (2001)

EC Competition Law (Second Edition, 1993), by Daniel G. Goyder

EC Competition Procedure (1996), by Luis Ortiz-Blanco

Antitrust Law and Economics in a Nutshell (Fourth Edition, 1994), by Ernest Gelhorn and William E. Kovacic

Antitrust (Third Edition, 1999), by Herbert Hovenkamp

Unfair Trade Practices in a Nutshell (Third Edition, 1993), by Charles R. McManis

Comparative Law of Monopolies (1996 with supplements), by David M. Raybould

I.C. Business Financing

A common saying is that "it takes money to make money". Business organizations need financial resources for several purposes—for example, to purchase the raw materials and the equipment used for manufacturing goods and to meet various overhead expenses (office accommodations, salaries of employees, etc.). The following paragraphs describe some of the more common ways such financial resources are obtained. These ways include the issuance of stock, the issuance of bonds (long-term debt obligations), the selling or pledging of accounts receivable (money owed to the company by its customers), the creation of security interests in movable property, and the use of commercial paper.[16]

I.C.1. Equity Financing (Stocks); Long-Term Debt Financing (Bonds)

A basic choice for a business entity wanting to raise additional financing is between (i) equity financing and (ii) debt financing. *Equity financing* comes from having additional investors enter as owners of the company, and of course providing money for doing so. *Debt financing*, in contrast, comes from borrowing money. Both methods have their drawbacks. In the case of equity financing, of course, the ownership interest of the original owners is diluted. In the case of debt financing, the business entity will need to pay interest and fees and be careful to repay the borrowed money on time in order to maintain its reputation as a creditworthy business entity.

Section A of this Chapter describes the ownership structures that exist in various forms of business organization. Of those forms, the stock company (or its common-law-system equivalent, the publicly-traded corporation) is most amenable to equity financing, because the company can issue additional ownership shares fairly easily. Doing so puts additional funds at the disposal of the company and usually carries with it no obligation to make any immediate payments, because the decision to declare dividends rests largely within the discretion of the company's board of directors. Typically, the issuance of additional ownership shares is subject to stringent legal requirements designed to ensure that the invitation to purchase the shares is accompanied by accurate information about the financial position of the company. As noted in section D of this Chapter, this is a key reason why standard accounting rules have been developed and adopted.

---

16. For more details on the forms of business financing, see Cameron, *supra* note 1, at pages 332–358. The following paragraphs draw from this source, as well as from others.

The issuance of ownership shares, and the trading of existing shares, often takes place (especially for large companies) in *stock markets*. The operations of a stock market, and the trades that take place there, are usually supervised and regulated by a government agency.

Similarly, the issuance by companies of long-term debt instruments is usually closely supervised by a government agency. Debt instruments—that is, documents that include written promises to repay money at some future date—can be short-term, medium-term, or long-term in maturity (the period at the end of which the money is to be repaid). Long-term debt instruments, usually over three years or so, are called "*bonds*". Such bonds can carry a number of different features:

- they can be issued in "registered form" (that is, to a particular person whose name appears on the bond itself), or in "bearer form" (that is, in a form that lets the ownership of the debt pass from one person to another without notifying the company that issued the bond);
- they can carry whatever maturity and interest rate and other terms the company decides on—although of course the company will try to set those terms in such a way that the bonds will be attractive enough to entice investors to buy them;
- they can be either (i) secured—that is, providing specific assets (often long-term assets such as land, buildings, and equipment) as collateral which the bond-holders can take control of and sell if the company fails to repay the debt—or (ii) unsecured, without such collateral being provided; and
- they can, in some systems, be put in "uncertificated form" (or "book-entry form")—that is, registered on the books of the company (and often in computerized form), instead of being evidenced by an actual document provided by the company to the creditor (the person buying the bond).

I.C.2. Short-Term Financing—Accounts Receivable; Security Interests

Bonds are used mainly by large companies. A form of financing that is available both to a large company and to a small company revolves around the "*accounts receivable*" of the company—that is, the amounts of money that are owed to the company (but have not yet been paid to it) by persons or other businesses to which the company has sold goods or provided services.

Financial transactions that rest on the basis of a company's accounts receivable are typically structured in one of two ways. First, the company may use the accounts receivable (as evidenced by documents) as collateral for a loan that the company gets from a bank. In that case, the company would collect on the accounts receivable as they come due and use those funds to pay off the bank loan. Second, the company can actually sell the accounts receivable to a bank for cash—that is, sell to the bank the right to collect on the accounts as they come due. Usually, of course, the bank will not pay the company the full value represented by the accounts receivable, since the bank is now taking on the risk that the person who owes the account will not pay it.

In the first case described above—using accounts receivable as collateral—the company will in some cases need to file a public notice that certain accounts receivable are being used as collateral in this way, in order that other creditors will be warned against providing further loans to the company on the basis of those same accounts receivable. In the second case—selling accounts receivable—the company typically will be required to notify the person who owes the money, so that that person will know that he or she is supposed to pay the bank, not the company.

Another form of short-term debt financing uses property of a company (often movable property, but also other types of property) as the collateral for a loan received by that company from a bank or other type of creditor. The key aims of laws on *securitized lending* of this sort (often discussed under the title "secured transactions") are (i) to provide the debtor with the right to enjoy maximum use of the debtor's movable property, thus keeping it in productive use, and (ii) to provide the creditor with an effective and efficient means of taking control of the movable property if the debtor defaults on the loan. Modern laws governing such securitized lending typically focus on the concept of a "charge" (or "security interest") created on movable property by the debtor in favor of the secured party (that is, the lender) to secure repayment of the debt. Such a charge is to be registered at a central registry that is indexed (for easy searching) and available for public review, so that future potential creditors will be in a position to know who (if anyone) has higher-priority claims over a debtor's movable property. The priority of any charge typically depends on the time of registration, with the earliest registration generally having the highest priority over other creditors.

In addition to the forms of short-term financing summarized above, various *other forms of short-term financing* are also available in many countries. One of these is factoring. "Factoring," (sometimes called "forfaiting") typically refers to a transaction in which a bank guarantees the promissory note issued by a buyer. This form of financing is especially attractive in the context of international sales of goods where the seller and buyer are not accustomed to doing business with each other and the seller wishes to reduce the risk of nonpayment from the buyer. In a factoring transaction, if the buyer fails to pay, then the bank will pay. Obviously the bank will need to be compensated for the risk that it assumes; accordingly, the bank will buy (from the seller) the promissory note (as issued by the buyer to the seller) at a discount. Somewhat similar to factoring is the use of "acceptances". These can be either "bankers' acceptances" or "trade acceptances". An acceptance is a promise by the drawee of a draft or bill of exchange that the instrument will be honored at maturity. A banker's acceptance is attractive to a seller (for example, an exporter of goods) because it results in the seller being paid immediately—that is, when a bank provides an "acceptance" it endorses a debt and provides the seller with immediate cash payment. A "trade acceptance" operates in the same manner, except that the entity providing the acceptance is a merchant rather than a bank. Yet another form of short-term financing comes from the work of venture capital companies and leasing companies. Because both of these types of entities will be subject to national laws, and those national laws vary greatly from one country to another, it is difficult to generalize about the operations of such companies. Typically, however, a venture capital company is an entity that provides either debt or equity financing for other business organizations, usually early in their existence or when they are undergoing an expansion of operations, in order to provide short-term budgetary and operational financing. Similarly, a leasing company is an entity that helps a business organization obtain the use of equipment without actually purchasing the equipment outright. Such a leasing arrangement leaves the business organization with more cash on hand and therefore constitutes a form of short-term financing.

I.C.3. Commercial Paper Financing

The laws relating to commercial paper are complex, in part because they are not always expressed by using the same sets of terms. For purposes of the following paragraphs, the relevant terms will carry the meanings shown in the definitions given by one writer[17] for the terms "bills of exchange" and "promissory note"—both of which are forms of "commercial paper". These definitions are consistent with most international usage.

> *Bill of exchange*: a written, dated, and signed three-party instrument containing an unconditional order by a drawer that directs a drawee to pay a definite sum of money to a payee on demand or at a specified future date.

> *Promissory note*: a written, dated, and signed two-party instrument containing an unconditional promise by a maker to pay a definite sum of money to a payee on demand or at a specified future date.

There are several kinds of bills of exchange. The kind most familiar to a consumer is a *check*, in which the drawee is a bank, and the drawer is a person who has money on deposit in that bank. When the drawer writes a check to another person drawn on the drawer's bank, that person (the payee) can take that check to the drawer's bank (the drawee), which will make the payment as directed. Alternatively, the payee can take the check to a different bank where the payee has a deposit and trigger a payment mechanism by which the funds will be transferred from the drawer's bank account to the payee's bank account.

---

17. August-1993, *supra* note 1, at page 539.

A detailed system of rules has been developed to govern the use of bills of exchange. The foundations for these rules date back several centuries. Until the middle of the seventeenth century, a single international law, the *Lex Mercatoria* (mercantile law, or "law merchant", or commercial law) applied in much of Europe. After that point, however, with the rise of independent nation-states in Europe, different rules were developed in various countries. Most recently, beginning early in the twentieth century, several efforts were made to return to a uniform set of rules. Those efforts culminated in 1930 with three treaties creating a Uniform Law on Bills of Exchange and Promissory Notes ("ULB") and in 1931 with two more treaties creating a Uniform Law for Checks. These rules were ratified by most countries in continental Europe, and today they serve, according to one writer, as "the standard laws governing bills of exchange and checks in virtually every nation, with the exception of the Anglo-American common law countries."[18] A harmonization between the common-law rules and the more widely accepted rules is expected to result from another treaty finalized in 1988 by the United Nations Commission on International Trade Law ("UNCITRAL"), called the Convention on International Bills of Exchange and International Promissory Notes. That treaty, which does not apply to checks, has not yet entered into force. UNCITRAL has also adopted the texts of several other treaties relating to international trade and finance.[19]

As the titles of these treaties indicate, they cover promissory notes as well as (most) bills of exchange. It is those promissory notes that form the basis for the type of "*commercial paper financing*" that this subsection refers to. A business entity may, by executing a promissory note, raise short-term funds for use in its operations. Typically, such a promissory note must have certain attributes to be easily marketable and achieve the results the business entity wants. For one thing, the promissory note must be negotiable—that is, transferable from one person to another (for value, of course). This makes the

---

18. *Id*. at pages 534–535.

19. For information about treaties prepared under the auspices of UNCITRAL, see www.uncitral.org. One of the most recent ones is the United Nations Convention on the Assignment of Receivables in International Trade (2001).

promissory note attractive as a basis for lending money. Indeed, if properly prepared, a negotiable promissory note can be almost as freely exchangeable as currency.

A common layout for such a promissory note (consistent with the 1988 UNCITRAL treaty referred to above) is evident from the following sample form:

International Promissory Note (*UNCITRAL Convention*)

__{ date }__   €_____
__{ place }__

__{ number of days, e.g., 90 }__ days after the above date, for value received, the undersigned maker promises to pay this promissory note to the order of __{ name of payee }__ at __{ place }__, the amount of __{ amount in words }__, with interest thereon from the date above at the rate of __{ percent }__ per annum payable at maturity.

_____
Maker

This sample form, when filled in, would include each of the key elements typically required of a negotiable promissory note. The most important of those elements (as required in both the 1930 ULB and the 1988 UNCITRAL Convention) are:

- that it be in writing
- that it be payable to order or to bearer
- that it contain the term "promissory note"
- that it state the place where drawn
- that it state the place where payable
- that it be dated
- that it state an unconditional promise or order to pay
- that it state a definite sum of money
- that it be payable on demand or at a definite time
- that it be signed by the maker

All of these elements are self-explanatory except the second one. Although a promissory note is commonly made payable "to the order of" a named person and is transferred to another person when the named person endorses (signs) the promissory note, a promissory note can also be made payable "to bearer", in which case it can be transferred merely by delivering it to another person (who is then the new "bearer" of it).

Further Readings on Business Financing

(in addition to the sources cited in the footnotes in this section)

International Securities Law Handbook (Second Edition, 2004), edited by Jean-Luc Soulier and Marcus Best

Securities Regulation in a Nutshell (Ninth Edition, 2006), by Thomas Lee Hazen and David L. Ratner

Black Letter on Negotiable Instrument (and Other Related Commercial Paper) (Second Edition, 1993), by Steve H. Nickles

The Law of Promissory Notes (Looseleaf, starting 1992), by Richard B. Hagedorn

Secured Transactions in a Nutshell (Fourth Edition, 2000), by Henry J. Bailey and Richard B. Hagedorn

A Basic Outline of the Law of Commercial Paper (1994), by Gerald J. Thain

I.D. Accounting Rules

In order for economic choices to be made intelligently, people need reliable information about costs and values. In the context of business organizations, accounting standards and practices have been developed to help provide such information. In fact, one legal scholar has noted that "[e]ach stage in the development of business associations has been associated with a new level of accounting sophistication."[20] Because the activities and structures of some business organizations are now highly complex, the task of accounting for their

---

20. Detlev F. Vagts, *Law and Accounting in Business Associations*, in INTERNATIONAL ENCYCLOPEDIA OF COMPARATIVE LAW (Vol. XIII, Ch. 12A), at page 4 (Oceana Publications, 1972). The following paragraphs draw heavily on this source, as well as from Charles H. Meyer, ACCOUNTING AND FINANCE FOR LAWYERS IN A NUTSHELL (West Publishing, 2d ed., 2002).

operations and their financial status has led to the development of very extensive and complicated rules. Adding to this complexity is the fact that detailed accounting rules and standards differ from one country to another. Currently, while there is no single, all-powerful accounting body that can promulgate accounting principles for all countries, the International Accounting Standards Board works toward harmonizing accounting around the world. Participants in the IASB agree on certain accounting methods and procedures that can then be adopted by local accounting setting bodies.[21]

Fortunately, it is possible to identify some key concepts and practices that are fairly straightforward and nearly universal in their acceptance. The following paragraphs explain those concepts, beginning with (1) a brief historical introduction that shows why business owners and others have insisted on the development of standard procedures and (2) an explanation of two key regulatory reasons for requiring business organizations to follow certain prescribed accounting rules. The discussion then turns to the most common accounting documents: the balance sheet and the income statement.

I.D.1. History of Accounting Rules — The Need for "Uniformity"

Accounting and capitalism have developed hand in hand. As trading houses and banking organizations in Europe started attracting outside investors several centuries ago, those outsiders demanded reliable information about the businesses they were investing in. An early treatise on accounting written in Italy in 1494 thus shows some of the emphasis then being placed on uniformity of treatment — that is, uniformity in the way financial matters were recorded and the way assets were valued, so that business decisions could be made intelligently.

The same demand — for reliable financial information through uniformity of accounting practices — appeared in northern Europe in the 17th and 18th centuries. As in Italy two centuries earlier, the rise of

---

21. See Meyer, *supra* note 20, at page 438.

large merchant companies with many investors led to the development of standardized procedures and accounting documents, including the balance sheet (discussed in subsection 3, below) to disclose the assets and liabilities of a company at a particular point in time.

This is easy to illustrate with a present-day example. Assume that a company named Cricket, Ltd. manufactures computers in Brussels. Assume further that Cricket, Ltd. has succeeded financially in the past two years and wants to expand its operations. In order to enable it to manufacture and sell twice as many computers, it might need to obtain more capital from outside investors. Assume also that Fudge Jones, from Zurich, has some money to invest. If he is prudent, Fudge Jones will not invest any money in Cricket, Ltd. without first obtaining information about the company's financial health. If there were no standard procedures used for recording the value of certain types of transactions and assets—if, for example, every company used a different system, or no system at all, in recording the value of the equipment it owned—Fudge Jones would not be (and should not be) confident enough to make an investment in Cricket, Ltd. Because Cricket, Ltd. and other companies need outside investors, standard accounting rules have developed.

Also at an early stage, governments in some countries imposed accounting requirements. An ordinance issued in France in 1673 attempted to force merchants to follow orderly record-keeping norms. That ordinance was related to the administration of bankruptcies (see Section E of this Chapter for a discussion of bankruptcy). Later, in the 19th century, government requirements took the form of legislation aimed at protecting shareholders in corporations, the numbers of which were then growing rapidly in some countries. At the same time, the rise of large manufacturing companies with substantial assets and inventories led to more sophisticated methods of assigning values to property, including calculations to reflect the declining market value of assets over time (depreciation) and fluctuations in the value and number of goods held by a company awaiting further processing or sale.

In all these developments, whether prompted by investors or by governments, a key demand was for "*uniformity*" in accounting practices. But the term "uniformity" can have more than one meaning in this context. For one thing, it can mean that all business organizations are required to use the same form of accounts—sometimes called a "chart of accounts"—with specific labels prescribed for each account. Under this type of *"format uniformity"*, every particular kind of payment—for example, a dividend to shareholders or a payment of taxes to the government or an installment on a loan—must appear on the financial records of every company in exactly the same way.

On the other hand, "uniformity" might mean that a particular method (as distinct from a particular format) be used. For example, if Cricket, Ltd., manufacturing computers in Brussels, has some computers still in its inventory (that is, not yet sold to customers) one year after they were made, and the company's cost of manufacturing computers has dropped substantially during that year, how should the cost of those unsold computers be recorded for accounting purposes? Different methods would seem to be possible (see below for a discussion of "LIFO" and "FIFO" methods). But *"method uniformity"* would require that all business organizations use the same single method for recording the value of the unsold computers.

Some accountants and business managers (and their lawyers) in many countries object to either "format uniformity" or "method uniformity" as described above. They claim that they should be permitted to use accounting methods and document formats of their own choosing, as long as the choices they make are reasonable in their particular type of operations. A third type of uniformity, however, is very widely accepted. This may be called *"uniformity over time"*. In general, a business organization should use the same method in one year as in the previous year for recording its economic activities; if it changes the method, it should clearly explain the difference and how it affects the relevant financial records and documents.

One noteworthy accounting challenge facing any business operating in foreign markets is foreign currency transactions. When a domestic business operates in a foreign market, it often engages in transactions that are denominated entirely in foreign currency. The challenge arises in converting the foreign currency into the domestic currency, either on the date the transaction occurs, or later, when the transaction is reported on a periodical financial statement.[22]

---

22. See *id.* at pages 424–437.

I.D.2. Dispositive Requirements and Disclosure Requirements

As noted above, governments have for a long time imposed rules regarding accounting. This is more true today than ever before. Generally speaking, there are two key types of regulatory requirements that give rise to such rules—what one legal scholar has called (i) the "dispositive" requirements and (ii) the "disclosure" requirements applicable to business organizations.[23]

Dispositive requirements may be described as those that require a company to take, or to refrain from taking, a particular kind of action if a certain financial situation exists. For example, a company may be prohibited from paying a dividend to its shareholders unless its assets or earnings exceed stated amounts; or a corporation may be required to declare bankruptcy if the level of its assets falls below the level of its liabilities. In such cases, of course, it is very important to know how to calculate the value of assets and liabilities.

Disclosure requirements are those that obligate a company's management to report periodically to its owners or to their representatives. These are designed mainly to enable the owners (for example, shareholders) to make collective decisions about the management of the company, or to make individual decisions about selling or buying interests in the company. But these periodic reports are also read by many others—government regulators, potential investors, and workers—who pass scrutiny on the company for various reasons.

Disclosure requirements have recently become especially demanding in many countries; particularly those that have operating within their borders many companies that are large and that engage in complex transactions. For example, businesses increasingly undertake transactions in "derivative financial instruments" such as futures and forward contracts, which frequently can help a business manage certain price risks and financial risks relating to a business' other assets and liabilities; but the potential risk associated with the "derivatives" themselves cannot always be articulated accurately on the business'

---

23. Vagts, *supra* note 20, at page 7.

financial statements.[24] Typically, a country's laws will try to overcome these difficulties by requiring more detailed disclosure. Moreover, a greater degree of disclosure, and hence usually more complicated accounting rules, will be prescribed for companies that reach a specified size, or whose shares are publicly traded. In contrast, the disclosure requirements, and therefore the accounting rules, are typically much less demanding for partnerships and single proprietorships.

A common type of disclosure requirement obligates a company to issue an *annual report* on its financial progress and condition. Other actions by a company—for example, listing shares on a stock exchange, or issuing securities to the public—can also trigger a special requirement for financial disclosure. In all such situations, the accounting practices must conform to certain standards.

I.D.3. Key Accounting Standards

The preceding paragraphs describe the historical and regulatory reasons that underlie the development of accounting standards. But what in fact are those standards? As noted above, the details differ from one country to another, but some are nearly universal. Four such standards are summarized below, setting the stage for an introduction to the two main accounting documents—the balance sheet and the income statement. The four standards are:

- the double-entry system
- objectivity
- the going-concern assumption
- inter-period consistency

The *double-entry system* of accounting developed centuries ago. It was clearly understood and used in Italy in the late 1400s. It turns on an equation usually expressed in this way: Assets = Liabilities + Ownership Equity. The equation can also be expressed as Assets = Liabilities + Net Worth, which can be restated as Assets − Liabilities = Net Worth. In all these equations, the underlying concept is that any business entity has

---

24. See Meyer, *supra* note 20, at pages 206–207.

assets (economic resources owned by the business entity, such as cash, merchandise, land, etc.) and, offsetting those assets, it has various types of liabilities (amounts owed by the enterprise to its creditors, including taxes owed to the government). The difference in value between the two (Assets – Liabilities) equals the amount of equity that the owners have in the business, or in other words its net worth.

The term "double-entry system" of accounting derives from the mechanism that has been developed for keeping track of transactions and values within the context of the basic equation described above. Traditionally, all transactions of a business are recorded in a "journal"—a chronological record of payments, receipts, and other transactions. In that journal, every transaction is recorded with two sets of entries—one or more "debit" entries and one or more "credit" entries. The total value of the debit entries equals the total value of the credit entries. Usually the debit entries are placed on the left-hand side of a two-column page in the journal, and the credit entries are placed on the right-hand side of the two-column page in the journal. By convention, debit or left-hand entries are used to show an increase in an asset account or a decrease in a liability or ownership equity account, and credit or right-hand entries are used to show a decrease in an asset account or an increase in a liability or ownership equity account.

As the equation above (Assets = Liabilities + Ownership Equity) suggests, a transaction can lead to any one of several possible sets of entries: an increase of one asset and a decrease in another; or an increase in both a liability and an asset; or an increase in an asset and an element of ownership; or any of the other permutations involving one or more of the three categories in the formula—so long as the equality is maintained.

The usual accounts within each of the three categories are listed below. The meanings of some are self-evident, and others will be discussed below in the context of the balance sheet.

Assets	Liabilities	Ownership
Cash	Notes Payable	Capital Stock
Accounts Receivable	Accounts Payable	Reserves & Provisions
Inventory	Tax	Retained Earnings (Earned Surplus)
Land & Buildings		
Plant & Equipment		
Intangible Assets		

Here is an illustration. If Cricket, Ltd. borrows €20 thousand (twenty thousand Euro) from a bank to expand the Cricket computer-making operations, the Cricket bookkeepers would add an amount of €20 thousand under the category of Liabilities-Notes Payable (because the bank would require a note from Cricket evidencing the loan) and would also add an amount of €20 thousand under the category of Assets-Cash (which includes demand deposits in banks). If Cricket then used €10 thousand in cash to purchase a new piece of equipment for its computer manufacturing operations, its bookkeepers would subtract an amount of €10 thousand under the category in Assets labeled Cash and would add an amount of €10 thousand under the category in Assets labeled Plant & Equipment.

A second common accounting standard is that of *objectivity*. In entering the amounts involved in the above example, there is little scope for subjective judgment to be made: the amounts provided in the loan and required for the purchase are definite because they involve movements of specific amounts of money. In many cases, however, there will be scope for subjectivity in assigning values. Assume, for example, that in mid-December, just before the end of its financial year, Cricket, Ltd. sells fifty computers to a buyer "on credit"—that is, on terms that require payment to be made not immediately but instead after three months. That transaction would be entered as a debit under the category Assets—Accounts Receivable and as a credit under the category Assets—Inventory. If, in early January (a few weeks after making the sale), Cricket, Ltd. discovers that the buyer is on the brink of bankruptcy and has failed to pay most of its bills to other suppliers, how should the value of the "account receivable" from the buyer be reflected in the Cricket annual financial reports? The managers of Cricket, Ltd. might still hope to receive payment, but they will of course need to base the valuation of the "account receivable" on more than mere hope. There is a need to treat the matter objectively: at some point the buyer's failure to pay will need to be reflected in a change in the value of the "account receivable". The aim is to assure that the Cricket accounts present a "true and fair view" of the financial condition of the business entity.

In preparing its annual financial statements—especially the balance sheet discussed a few paragraphs below—Cricket, Ltd. will be catching in motion, at one point in time, a set of ongoing operations in various stages of completion. Put differently, the periodic reports of a business entity take a non-moving picture of a quickly changing scene. The *going-concern assumption* means that in valuing assets and liabilities for purposes of that non-moving picture, it should be assumed that the business entity will continue its operations. The alternative approach would be to value assets and liabilities as if the business were going to be wound up immediately. If that were the case, of course, the value of many of the company's assets would be much lower, since their main value is in the productive capacity they have for that particular business enterprise, rather than in any resale value they could bring if they had to be liquidated (sold for cash) on short notice. In normal circumstances, therefore, the valuation of items in the company's accounts should be made on the basis of the going-concern assumption. If, by contrast, the company faces bankruptcy, this assumption disappears; then the market value on a sudden sale would have to be used for valuation purposes.

The standard of *inter-period consistency* is mentioned above as a form of "uniformity", but it bears repeating. A business entity should use the same principles and approaches in its bookkeeping and preparation of financial statements in one year as in previous years. Otherwise it is difficult to make any useful comparison between years regarding the performance and condition of the business entity. It is tempting, of course, for a company to use sleight of hand in adjusting values of accounts in any particular year, in order to yield financial statements that it considers most favorable. For the most part, accounting rules require that this temptation be resisted.

In addition to the four key accounting standards summarized above—double-entry, objectivity, "going-concern", and inter-period consistency—we should also take note of another standard practice or convention: conservatism. In the accounting context, conservatism means that whenever there is uncertainty about the value of an asset or the appropriateness of recording a particular transaction, that uncertainty "will be resolved with a 'bias' in favor of understating income or assets."[25]

I.D.4. The Balance Sheet and the Income Statement

The two key financial accounting documents in most systems are the balance sheet and the income statement (sometimes called the profit-and-loss statement). The first of these presents a picture of the financial condition of the business entity—that is, the values of its assets and the claims against it—as of a particular point in time, usually at the end of a financial year. The second provides an overview of the main categories of expenditure and revenue during a specified period.

The *balance sheet* carries that label because it reflects the basic equation mentioned above: Assets = Liabilities + Ownership Equity. This oversimplifies the complexity of most balance sheets, but it is generally true. The balance sheet is constructed with assets listed on one side, and a total figure at the bottom, and liabilities and components of ownership and related accounts on the other side. The total of liabilities and ownership equals the total of assets. The accounts within the three main categories are as listed above, and they would typically appear in a (simplified) balance sheet as shown below.

BALANCE SHEET Cricket, Ltd. as of 31 December 2007 (in € thousands, rounded)			
Assets		**Liabilities**	
Cash	120	Current Liabilities	1,880
Accounts Receivable	260	Long-Term Debt	520
Inventory	890	Other Liabilities & Reserves	210
Land & Buildings	2,850	*Total Liabilities*	2,610
Plant & Equipment	1,330	**Stockholders' Equity**	
Other Assets	440	Capital Stock	340
		Paid-In Surplus	500
Total Assets	5,890	Retained earnings	2,440
		Total St.Eq.	3,280
		Total Liab. & Stock. Equity	5,890

25. *Id.* at page 63.

The Cash account was discussed briefly above. The Accounts Receivable account includes amounts owing to the company as a result of having furnished goods or services to others, with payment not yet having been received. Usually, an item is not included in this account unless the company has already supplied all of the goods or services, or nearly so. As suggested above, an important question in some cases is whether the amount of an item in the Accounts Receivable account should be reduced because of the possibility that it will not be paid. That question is often a matter of subjective judgment, or even conjecture.

The Inventory account includes the value of goods held for sale in the ordinary course of business, and also might include goods that are in the process of being manufactured. How should such goods (whether completed or not) be valued? As a general rule, the value is (i) the cost of production (or acquisition) of the article or (ii) the current market value of the article, whichever is lower. Another question arises from the fact that items in inventory come and go and are difficult to account for individually. Assume, for example, that the Cricket, Ltd. computer company manufacturers a thousand computers during 2006, but the cost of manufacturing them fluctuates during the year between €1,700 per computer and a minimum of €1,300 each. If the pace of the company's sales of computers also fluctuates over time, it will be nearly impossible to match the sale price of each computer with the cost of production of that computer. Several methods have been devised to avoid this difficulty. One is the "*FIFO*" (first-in-first-out) method, in which goods are deemed to have been sold in the order in which they were produced or acquired. Another is the "*LIFO*" (last-in-first-out) system, in which the most recently produced or acquired goods are deemed to have been sold first. A third is the "average cost" method, in which the average cost of producing or acquiring goods through the preceding period is used for calculating the value of inventory remaining at the end of the period. Inflation affects the values differently, depending on which method is used.

Land, buildings, plant, and equipment may be referred to as "*fixed assets*". A key question regarding the valuation of them for accounting purposes is whether the cost of acquiring them is a measure of their current value. Usually it is not, so various methods of revaluing such assets have been devised. In most circumstances, such assets are assumed to depreciate over time (that is, their value is assumed to have fallen). Because it is difficult to engage in periodic re-determinations of the market value of such an asset, a system is usually used for gradually "writing off" its value (that is, reducing it to zero) over the course of a period of years that reflects the expected life of the asset.

The "*Other Assets*" account might include the value of investments that the company being reported on has in other companies. It might also include "intangible assets"—value that is thought to have been created for the company through research, through the costs of building up a strong organization, and in the way of "good will" or customer appeal. Although it is often undisputed that these intangible items do have value, it is just as often difficult to establish with any certainty at all what that value is.

The accounts on the Liabilities side of the balance sheet are often easier to value than those on the Assets side. In this context the term "*liability*" means a presently existing, recognized obligation to pay a given amount. Often a company's liabilities are divided into (i) Current Liabilities, such as accounts payable (payments due on contracts under which suppliers have already made delivery) and taxes payable during the year, (ii) Long-Term Debt on which payment is not due within a prescribed period (one year in some systems, up to four in others), and (iii) Other Liabilities and Reserves, a category that reflects the fact that amounts will probably or surely be due in the future for such items as employees' pension payments.

Under the Shareholder's Equity category, the various entries carry these meanings: Capital Stock represents the amount of the stated value ("par value") per share times the number of shares that have been issued; Paid-In Surplus represents the amount contributed by shareholders buying shares at a price in excess of the par value; and Retained Earnings is the account representing the funds that the company's managers have decided to keep in the business and not to distribute, in order to strengthen or expand it.

Whereas the balance sheet presents a picture of the financial condition of a company at a particular point in time (in fact, it is occasionally referred to as the "statement of financial position"), the *income statement* provides a summary of the changes that have taken place within the period to which it refers—usually a one-year period but in some companies quarterly or semi-annually as well. The income statement is important in large part because it represents the capacity to produce earnings and dividends, which is a matter of crucial importance to long-term investors.

An income statement usually follows one of two basic formats. In one, items of expense are shown on one side and items of revenue are shown on the other side. The net income of the company appears as the difference between the two totals. In the other format, there is only one column. It starts with gross revenue and subtracts various types of expenses from that amount, culminating in a net income figure. A simplified income statement (which, as noted above, is sometimes called a "profit-and-loss statement" or a "statement of results of operations") appears below:

INCOME STATEMENT Cricket, Ltd. 1 January to 31 December 2007 (in € thousands, rounded)		
Revenue from Sales		695
Costs and expenses		
Cost of goods sold	(280)	
Depreciation of assets	(46)	
Selling & administrative costs	(51)	
Employee retirement plans	(35)	
Total costs and expenses		(412)
Taxes		(82)
Net Income		201

The item labeled "Revenue from Sales" represents payments made to the business entity for goods it has produced and sold. In the case of an entity providing services, instead of goods, the item would more likely be labeled "Revenue from Operations". Sometimes another form of revenue might be included under the label of "Other Gains", which would include the results of transactions that occur other than in the ordinary course of business—for example, from the sale of a piece of equipment or a vehicle owned by the business entity. If an unusual transaction such as this results in a loss, it might be included under the label of "Extraordinary Losses".

All the other items included in the sample income statement provided above are to be subtracted from Revenues. That is why the figures for Costs and Expenses and for Taxes appear in parentheses. If it happens that the sum of the Costs and Expenses and Taxes exceeds the amount of Revenues, then there will be a Net Loss (with figures appearing in parentheses) instead of a Net Income.

As noted above, the balance sheet and the income statement are two very common types of financial statements. Other types of financial statements are also sometimes prepared, or even required. These include: (i) a *statement of owner's equity*, summarizing changes that took place in the Ownership Equity accounts during a particular period (usually one year); and (ii) a *statement of cash flows*, providing details about the changes in the business entity's cash balance during a particular period. (Note: Income does not equal cash; a business entity can be earning income and yet be suffering from a shortage of cash—either because some of the income takes the form of accounts receivable instead of cash, or because cash is being used to replace assets or to expand the entity's operations.) In all of these financial statements, supplementary and explanatory information will appear as Notes—explaining, for example, what accounting methods have been used for calculating the amount of depreciation or the value of inventories.

In some cases, special explanations will also have to be provided in connection with financial statements reflecting the operation of a business engaged in transactions involving more than one national currency. Two issues are especially noteworthy in this regard.

The first is this: how should transactions that involve foreign currency be reflected in the business' accounting records? This issue can be especially important if those records are closed (and financial statements are prepared) when the business still holds some of the foreign currency—the value of which will typically continue to fluctuate, of course, in terms of the business' own national currency. Although many exceptions exist, the general rule is that an adjustment is made to reflect the exchange rate between the two currencies as of the end of the reporting period.

The second related issue is this: how should financial statements for a business that maintains its financial records in one currency be "translated" into another currency? (Such "translation" is often required, for example, if a company is subject to governmental regulation in more than one country, as would be the case if it is incorporated in Country A but is owned substantially by a parent company that is incorporated in Country B.) The rules for making such a "translation" of financial statements are quite complex and depend largely on national government regulations. One approach is to express the company's assets, liabilities, revenues, and expenses in the currency the regulating country based on the currency exchange rate that applies on the date as of which the financial statements are issued but to express the value of a parent company's investment in that foreign operation to reflect the currency exchange rate that was in effect on the date on which the investment was made.[26]

Further Readings on Accounting Rules

(in addition to the sources cited in the footnotes in this section)

Law and Accounting in Business Associations (1967 and 1972) (in Vol. XIII, Ch. 12A of International Encyclopaedia of Comparative Law), by Detlev F. Vagts

Basic Accounting for Lawyers (Fifth Edition, 1999), by Anthony Phillips and Richard W. Nicholson

Meyer's Accounting and Finance for Lawyers in a Nutshell (Second Edition, 2002), by Charles H. Meyer

I.E. Bankruptcy

I.E.1. Aim and Scope of Bankruptcy Law

Bankruptcy law provides a mechanism for dealing with a business entity (or any person) that is experiencing severe financial difficulties. According to one author, "bankruptcy law has two major pur-

---

26. *Id.* at page 434.

poses: to give the debtor a fresh start, and to provide equal treatment to creditors with the same types of claims."[27]

Beyond these general features, however, the specific rules on bankruptcy can vary significantly from one legal system to the next. They can also vary within one legal system depending on the character of the person or entity that is bankrupt. Banks, for example, are often subject to different rules from those applicable to other business entities because of the special role that banks play in a country's economy. [28]

I.E.2. Common Themes and Concepts

Despite the diversity in laws around the world, a few general observations can be made regarding bankruptcy. These relate to: (i) the situations that can trigger the commencement of bankruptcy proceedings; (ii) the immediate effects of commencing such proceedings; (iii) the difference between bankruptcies culminating in liquidation and those designed to reorganize a business entity; (iv) the mechanism by which a bankrupt debtor's assets are seized, sold, and distributed in a liquidation proceeding; and (v) the role of a "conservator" in a business reorganization.

Commencement of bankruptcy proceedings typically can be triggered by a debtor voluntarily, or by one or more creditors. Usually bankruptcy takes place only if the debtor is insolvent. Insolvency may be defined in various ways, but such definitions typically include both (i) a situation in which the debtor's liabilities exceed the debtor's assets and (ii) a situation in which the debtor is not able to pay debts as they come due.

Once a bankruptcy proceeding has been initiated, creditors are usually prohibited from taking any further steps to collect outstanding claims against the debtor. The key questions relating to such a restraint, sometimes referred to as an *"automatic stay"*, are (i) when

---

27. Cameron, *supra* note 1, at page 379. The following paragraphs draw from this source and others.

28. For a reference to bank insolvency, see "Other Issues in Banking and Monetary Law", in subsection C.3 of Chapter II.

does the automatic stay become effective, (ii) what is covered by the automatic stay, (iii) when does the automatic stay end, and (iv) how can a creditor obtain relief from the stay?[29] These questions are answered somewhat differently, of course, in different legal systems.

Bankruptcy can lead to a *liquidation proceeding*. Such a proceeding typically involves the appointment of a person to prepare an inventory of the debtor's assets, take control over those assets (subject to certain exceptions for personal property), sell the seized assets, and then distribute the proceeds to the creditors.

In a great many cases, of course, there will not be adequate proceeds to pay all the creditors in full. At that point the issue of *priority* arises. Some creditors' claims are almost surely given priority over others. For example, a creditor to whom specific property has been pledged as collateral for a loan will in most cases have priority over any other creditor in respect of the proceeds from the sale of that specific property. Likewise, priority is often given to a person or entity that extends credit or provides goods and services to keep a business entity in operation just following the initiation of the bankruptcy. Where several creditors having the same priority cannot all be paid in full, the law will typically provide for *pro rata* payments.

At the conclusion of the liquidation, the debtor will be *discharged* (excused) from any further liability on the debts involved in the bankruptcy proceeding, with some important exceptions; these usually include taxes and fines due to the government, or liability for money obtained by fraud or false pretenses, or liability to creditors whom the debtor intentionally failed to inform of the bankruptcy proceeding.

Bankruptcy might also lead to a different outcome in the case of a debtor business: *reorganization* of the business enterprise. Whereas a liquidation is similar to a death, reorganization is similar to a rehabilitation or a resurrection. The aim in such a case is to overcome a temporary and curable financial problem by imposing a temporary suspension of debt obligations while the business is being reorgan-

---

29. David G. Epstein, DEBTOR-CREDITOR LAW (West Publishing, 3rd ed. 1985), at page 160.

ized in a way that will permit it to return to financial health and then pay off those obligations in full. This would, it is thought, be less disruptive to the economy (especially to the local economy where the business operates and where its workers live) than a liquidation. Sometimes such a reorganization will take place under the business entity's own (pre-bankruptcy) managers; that is, they remain in control of the company's operations. In other cases, the bankruptcy law will require the appointment of a "conservator"—a person who will be responsible for turning around the fortunes of the business entity within a prescribed period of time. If those efforts fail, in many cases the business then will face liquidation as described above.

I.E.3. Cross-Border Insolvency

International bankruptcy, sometimes also called cross-border insolvency, has become a more important issue as businesses have become increasingly multinational.[30] In Europe, for example, nations may follow two different models of law when dealing with a multinational business' cross-border insolvency: the *territorial model* and the *universal model.*

In the territorial model, in each nation where the debtor has assets, that nation handles the insolvency according to its own law. The insolvency proceedings only concern the assets within the nation's territory; furthermore, only creditors from that nation may participate in the proceedings. The disadvantage of this model is that there can be many insolvency proceedings occurring simultaneously in every different nation where the debtor operated his or her business.[31]

In contrast, in the universal model, a single insolvency proceeding is held in the debtor's "home" nation. The same insolvency law applies to both procedural and substantive issues. The proceeding concerns all the debtor's assets and activities from every nation in

---

30. See Miguel Virgós & Francisco Garcimartín, THE EUROPEAN INSOLVENCY REGULATION: LAW AND PRACTICE (2004), at page 3.

31. See *id.* at page 11.

which the debtor operated his or her business—and all creditors, both national and foreign, may participate. However, the disadvantage of this model is that foreign creditors and nations are forced to recognize the "home" nation's final judgment and settlement of the debtor's insolvency.[32] Sometimes these two contrasting approaches to cross-borders insolvency can be combined or compromised. One commentator describes "modified universalism" as one type of such compromise:

> Modified universalism accepts the central premise of universalism, that assets should be collected and distributed on a worldwide basis, but reserves to local courts discretion to evaluate the fairness of the home-country procedures and to protect the interests of local creditors. When the local court decides to defer, deference may be general and unconditional or may be limited and conditioned upon certain developments in the [bankruptcy case]. Once the local court has determined to defer, however, substantial local assets may be turned over to the home-country court, or placed at its disposal, and local creditors may be dispatched to the home-country court to pursue their claims and resolve disputes.[33]

Further Readings on Bankruptcy Law

(in addition to the sources cited in the footnotes in this chapter)

Bankruptcy and Other Debtor-Creditor Law in a Nutshell (Fifth Edition, 1995), by David G. Epstein

Hornbook on Bankruptcy (1993), by David G. Epstein, Steve H. Nickles, and James J. White

Fundamentals of Bankruptcy Law (2006), by Richard B. Levin

---

32. *Id.* at page 12.

33. American Law Institute, *International Statement of United States Bankruptcy Law—Tentative Draft* (April 15, 1997) (prepared in connection with the "Transnational Insolvency Project" of the American Law Institute), at page 108.

Current Developments in International and Comparative Corporate Insolvency Law (1995), edited by Jacob S. Ziegel

Butterworths International Insolvency Laws (1994), edited by Philip Wood, Peter G. Totty, and Martin Bates

The European Insolvency Regulation: Law and Practice (2004), by Miguel Virgós and Francisco Garcimartín

Chapter II

Key Transactional Aspects of Business Operations

Chapter I focused on business entities, giving special attention to how they are created and structured, how they obtain and account for their financial resources, how they are dealt with when they face severe financial difficulties, and so forth. This Chapter II takes a different perspective: it explores the actual transactional operations of business entities—including some specialized types of business entities—in society.

This chapter opens with an examination of commercial transactions—that is, the buying and selling of goods and services. It then looks at various mechanisms that exist in most countries for resolving the disputes that can arise from such commercial transactions. Then two specialized types of business operations—banking and insurance, both of which are of central importance in modern economies—are summarized. The chapter ends with two topics that have gained dramatically in significance in just the last few years with advances in technology: intellectual property and cyber law.

II.A. Contract Law and Commercial Law

Contract law is a basic element of any legal system. The legal enforceability of certain promises forms the backbone of an economy. This section introduces five key aspects of contract law in general:

(1) formation of contracts; (2) validity of contracts; (3) interpretation of contracts; (4) performance, non-performance, and termination of contracts; and (5) remedies for breach of contract. Lastly it identifies some special features of the laws governing commercial contracts—that is, contracts for the sale of goods and services.

II.A.1. Contract Formation

In most developed legal systems, and in recent multilateral agreements dealing with contract law principles, the formation of a contract requires two elements: (i) an offer, plus (ii) an acceptance of that offer. For example, if Sun Yat-sen (Mr. Sun) says to Moon Soo-chung (Ms. Moon) "I will sell you this book for 50 won[34] and if Ms. Moon replies to Mr. Sun "I accept your offer", then a contract is formed.

In many cases, of course, two people will not speak that way. They will not make their offer and acceptance so obvious. Therefore, rules have developed to determine when the behavior of one person constitutes an offer and when the behavior of another person constitutes an acceptance.

Generally speaking, an *offer* has been made if one person indicates to another person, with a reasonable degree of clarity, either by spoken or written words or by behavior, that he or she is willing to enter into a binding promise to do a particular thing in return for that other person's doing or promise to do a particular thing.[35] Thus, an

---

34. The won is the national currency of Korea. Although the names I have used in this example are names of real people, the transaction is unlikely to occur, because Sun Yat-sen was a national leader in China in the early part of the twentieth century, after the fall of the Qing Dynasty in 1911. Moon Soo-chung is a friend of mine, and former colleague, from Korea—and male, not female as in my example.

35. One definition of an "offer" is a "manifestation of willingness to enter into a bargain, so made as to justify another person in understanding that his assent to that bargain is invited and will conclude it." *Second Restatement of Contracts* [USA], quoted in Gordon Schaber and Claude Rohwer, CONTRACTS IN A NUTSHELL (West Publishing, 1984). The following paragraphs draw from the Schaber and Rohwer book, as well as from Whitman and Gergacz, *supra* note 11.

offer has almost surely been made if Mr. Sun, while wearing a vender's permit and standing at a booth marked "Books for Sale", holds up a book to Ms. Moon as she walks by and says "50 won?" and shows a questioning look in his eyes. He need not actually say "I will sell you this book for 50 won." Unless a reasonable person would know that Mr. Sun is just joking and that no offer was intended, an offer has been made.

It is easy to imagine closer cases, in which reasonable people might have different interpretations of Mr. Sun's behavior. If he were not standing at a book-selling booth but instead were engaged in a conversation with Ms. Moon while walking down the street, he might hold up a book and say "50 won?" as an abbreviated way of saying any number of very different things—such as "Can you believe I spent 50 won for this little book?" or "Do you think I should sell this book to my neighbor for 50 won?" or "Would you like to buy this book from me for 50 won?" or something else. In such ambiguous cases it will be difficult to determine whether an offer has been made or not. However, the existence of close cases does not erode the general principle as stated in the first sentence of the paragraph before this one.

Similar rules apply to *acceptances*. Generally speaking, an offer has been accepted if the person to whom the offer has been made (the offeree) has indicated to the person making the offer (the offeror), with a reasonable degree of clarity, either by spoken or written words or by behavior, that the offeree is willing to do the thing requested by the offer. Thus, Ms. Moon can accept an offer made by Mr. Sun by any of several means—by saying "OK", or by making movements with her head or hands signaling that she is willing to pay the 50 won, or by actually holding out the 50 won for Mr. Sun to take. As in the case of offers, it is sometimes not completely clear whether an acceptance has been made. If such a case must be decided by application of legal procedures, a court will usually examine all the circumstances closely to see how the general rule stated above should apply in the particular facts of the case.

Detailed rules often exist regarding such things as: (i) duration of an offer (how long it is valid for a person to accept it); (ii) withdrawal of an offer (when an offer, once made, can be withdrawn) or of an acceptance; (iii) the degree to which an acceptance must match the terms of the offer in order for a contract to be formed; and (iv) the effect of rejection of an offer (it sometimes is viewed as constituting a "counteroffer" which the original offeror is then free to accept). These rules vary from one legal system to another, and they often vary depending on whether the contract is a contract for the commercial sale of goods or another kind of contract (for example, a contract for services, or a contract for the sale of land, or a contract not involving people or business entities involved in commerce).[36]

In many legal systems, certain types of contracts must be put in writing in order to be enforceable. These sometimes include contracts that cannot be performed within a specified period of time (for example, one year) and contracts involving the sale or lease of land. Similarly, in some legal systems, contracts for the sale of goods valued at over a specified amount must be put in writing.

Moreover, it is worth pointing out that in some legal systems— particularly those influenced by English common law—another element, called "consideration", must be shown to exist before a contract is formed as a legal matter. In English law, "consideration" is anything of value (an item or a service) which each party to a contract must agree to exchange. In other words, a contract must be "met with" or "supported by" consideration in order to be enforceable. The rules in US law are closely related but slightly different. In that system, "consideration" is something that is done or promised in return for a contractual promise. In order to meet the requirement that consideration be present (for a contract to be binding), three elements must be shown: (i) there must be a bargain regarding the terms of an exchange; (ii) there must be a mutual exchange; and (iii) the exchange must be of something having value. As can be seen from even this most abbreviated of explanations, the doctrine of "consideration" is quite complicated. Perhaps partly because of its complexity, it is absent from many legal systems.

---

36. For a survey of national legal regimes governing contract formation, see Arthur T. von Mehren, *The Formation of Contracts*, in INTERNATIONAL ENCYCLOPEDIA OF COMPARATIVE LAW (Vol. VII, Ch. 9) (Oceana Publications, 1992).

II.A.2. Contract Validity

If an offer has been made and accepted according to the rules summarized above, then a contract exists. Generally speaking, the law requires that a contract, once made, must be performed in accordance with its terms. This general rule is subject to *exceptions*. Some important exceptions fall under the heading of "contract validity". (Note: the terms "contract validity" and "contract enforceability" are often used interchangeably.)

A contract is usually not valid, and therefore not fully binding and enforceable, if one of the parties to it did not have the proper legal "*capacity*" to enter into it. For example, a ten-year-old boy would in most cases be seen as not having the legal capacity to enter into a contract for the sale of land or for the purchase of an automobile. Hence, a contract he enters into for such a purpose would not be enforceable against him by the other party. Specific legal rules usually govern what persons in the society have legal capacity. These rules are designed mainly to protect classes of people in the society whose maturity or mental abilities are considered inadequate to require them to be bound by contractual promises that they make.

Similarly, a contract is not enforceable if there has been some serious *misrepresentation* associated with its conclusion. For example, if Mr. Sun, wanting to sell a house to Ms. Moon, tells her that it has a good roof, or if he paints over some stains in order to hide the fact that the roof leaks, Ms. Moon would not usually be required to pay the purchase price if, having accepted his offer of sale, she then finds that the roof leaks. Likewise, if Mr. Sun forges documents claiming that a painting he wants to sell Ms. Moon was painted by a famous painter, Ms. Moon will in most cases not be required to pay the purchase price if, after accepting the offer, she discovers that the painting is by Mr. Sun himself.

Similarly, a contract may be declared unenforceable if *duress* was involved in the contract formation. An example would be a case in which one party threatens to burn down a second party's house unless that second party agrees to enter into a contract with the first party.

In some cases, a contract will not be enforced if, at the time the contract was concluded, its terms were so unfair as to make it "*unconscionable*" (in whole or in part) to hold one party to the bargain.

Of course, the fundamental principle on which contract law is founded is that persons are, and should be, free to make whatever bargains they want. Therefore, in many legal systems, the authority of a court to declare that a contract is unenforceable on account of its "unconscionability" will be very limited. On the other hand, modern economic life involves many situations in which the bargaining power between the parties is unequal, leading to great temptation on the part of some contracting parties to impose bargains on weaker parties that "no man in his senses would make, and that no honest and fair man would accept".[37] The rarity of such cases in a particular legal system will depend on how strong the "freedom of contract" doctrine is in that legal system. Under the "freedom of contract" doctrine (sometimes referred to as the "sanctity of contract" doctrine), contracting parties should be held to their promises for future performance in nearly all cases because the main purpose of a contract is to permit the parties to specify by mutual agreement who should bear certain risks and costs notwithstanding future events.

II.A.3. Contract Interpretation

Many contracts are made without much formality or attention to detail. Most people enter into hundreds of contracts in a year—buying vegetables, taking a taxicab, and the like. Most of those contracts are unwritten. Even when written, a contract can never specify precisely what every term means, and how it is to be construed in every conceivable circumstance. As a result, questions sometimes arise about just what the parties agreed to, or what they should be deemed to have agreed to—in short, how to interpret and apply the contract.

There are several *theories of contract interpretation*, especially in the case of written contracts. Under one such theory, a judgment about how to apply a contract should be made by examining only the words of the contract itself, and how a reasonable person would construe them, without any reference to other evidence that might show

---

37. This language is paraphrased from language quoted in Schaber and Rohwer, *supra* note 35, at page 179.

what the parties intended in the particular circumstances that have prompted a dispute. Under another theory, a judgment about how to apply a contract should be made after reviewing not only the contract itself but all other relevant information, such as the behavior of the parties, including prior courses of dealing, up to the time of the contract. Under another theory, the well-being of the parties, and perhaps even the values and priorities of the community as a whole, should be considered in determining how to interpret and enforce a contract.

Sometimes important terms of a contract are in effect added to it by outside parties, such as by judges or through legislation. This is essentially what happens when a law requires, for example, that certain specified terms (providing for specific warranties, for example) shall be deemed to be part of any contract for the sale of goods or provision of services, or for the sale of land. Similarly, when a court determines that a certain term is an "*implied term*" of a contract, the court is in many cases simply "filling in blanks" that the parties either did not consider or could not agree on during the formation of the contract. And another type of "implied term" that contract law imposes in many legal systems is a duty of good faith and fair dealing in the performance of every contract.

II.A.4. Contract Performance, Non-Performance, and Termination

Once a contract is formed, and assuming it is not unenforceable because of some form of invalidity, it is to be performed according to its terms as properly interpreted. What should happen if one party to the contract does not perform, or only performs part of the obligations that party has undertaken in the contract? Again, special rules govern such situations. In some cases, *partial performance* by one party has the result of reducing the obligation of the other party. In some cases, a total non-performance by one party is excused under the doctrine of "*force majeure*". That doctrine provides that if a circumstance of nature—sometimes called an "act of God"—takes place that makes performance impossible, the non-performance will be excused.

If there is no excuse for non-performance by one party, that non-performance will usually trigger the availability of *remedies* to the other party to the contract. These are discussed in subsection A.5, below.

In some cases, the non-performance by one party is so complete that it brings the contract to an end. In most cases (and assuming there is no excuse, as by means of *force majeure*), such a "*fundamental breach*" typically relieves the other party of all obligations under the contract, usually in addition to giving that other party the right to sue for compensation—often referred to as "monetary damages". Of course, a contract can also be terminated by mutual consent of the parties.

II.A.5. Remedies for Breach of Contract

As noted immediately above, a fundamental breach typically triggers a right on the part of the non-breaching party to sue for "monetary damages". This is the term used in many legal systems in referring to financial compensation owed by one party to another. The obligation to provide financial compensation occurs not only in the case of a fundamental breach but also in a range of other cases in which one party failed to fulfill the contract as promised.

Let us consider an illustration: If a painter promises to paint a person's entire house, including a small outside wall, and then the painter paints everything except the small wall, the remedy available to the owner of the house will typically be monetary compensation, or "damages". In a typical case, the painter would owe the owner of the house a sum of money that is equal to the value of the non-performance—the purpose being "to arrive at the same situation as if the contract had been performed".[38]

Detailed rules apply to the calculation of proper damages to be paid to the non-breaching party, especially if the non-performance causes other injury or economic loss to the other party. These rules

---

38. Michael H. Whincup, Contract Law and Practice—The English System and Continental Comparisons (Kluwer, 1990), at page 252 (describing the purpose of an award of damages under Dutch law).

will vary, of course, from one country to another. In many cases, however, the method of calculating the amount of "money damages" that a breaching party owes to the non-breaching party is the so-called "expectation measure of damages". One authority offers this summary of it:

> The fundamental goal in awarding contract damages is to put the promisee in as good a position as he or she would have been in had the promissor kept the promise. One way to do that is to apply the expectations measure of damages, which follows a three-step approach: ...
>
> (1) Determine the position the promisee would have been in if the promise had been kept. We call this the "promise-kept position."
>
> (2) Determine the position of the promisee as a result of the breach. We call this "the-result-of-breach position."
>
> (3) Award the difference in value (measured in money) between the promise-kept position and the-result-of-the-breach position.
>
> Awarding the difference in value (measured in money) between the promise-kept position and the-result-of-the-breach position achieves this goal to the extent that the promise-kept position plus money is equivalent to the promise-kept position.[39]

In some cases it might not be possible to use the "expectations measure of damages". If that is the case, the compensation awarded to a non-breaching party might be determined on another basis. One such basis is the "reliance measure", the aim of which is to restore the injured party to the economic position that that party had occupied at the time the contract was entered into. Another such basis is "restitution", the aim of which is to prevent the breaching party from being unjustly enriched.

Detailed rules also govern the requirement of mitigation—that is, to what extent a party to a contract should take steps to minimize the loss occurring as a result of another party's non-performance.

---

39. David M. Hull, *Contracts Remedies: The Expectations Measure of Damages*, available at http://www.lawstudysystems.com.

The discussion of "money damages" above focuses on one of the two principal types of remedies that a country's laws might make available to a party who has been injured in some way by the failure of the other party to perform a contract as promised. The other main possible type of remedy is "specific performance". This type of remedy is especially important in English common law, having emerged out of the historical peculiarities of the system of "equity" that arose there in the 14th and 15th centuries. The remedy of "specific performance", instead of merely compensating the non-breaching party, actually forces the breaching party to go forward with performance of the contract even though that party does not wish to do so. In actual practice, this remedy would most appropriately apply in cases regarding land. That is, if a seller of land refuses to convey title to a buyer as promised in a contract, then a court might, under the doctrine of "specific performance", require the owner to convey title.

In many countries that are most influenced by European civil law, "specific performance" is not available. In those countries, "monetary damages" will be the typical remedy for breach of contract.

II.A.6. Commercial Contracts

What is meant by the term "commercial contracts"? Definitions differ among legal systems and even within legal systems. In any definition, the central core of "commercial contracts" would be contracts for the sale of goods by merchants—that is, by persons who are in the business of selling goods. Some definitions of "commercial contracts" are broader; they include not only the sale of goods by merchants (either to consumers or to other merchants) but also the sale of services (for example, banking services or financial consulting services) by persons in the business of providing such services. Some definitions of "commercial contracts" are wider still, encompassing sales of real property such as office buildings or land.

At the heart of "commercial contracts", however, are contracts for the sale of goods by merchants. The following discussion focuses on such contracts; but it is important to bear in mind that the observations made below regarding commercial contracts involving goods will often apply as well, with certain adjustments, to contracts for the sale of services or of real property.

The law governing commercial contracts obviously forms a subset of the law governing contracts in general, discussed in the preceding paragraphs. However, certain special features have developed in the law of commercial contracts that warrant separate discussion. Indeed, these special features are of such importance that commercial contracts have in many countries, and internationally, been the subject of separate laws and codes. Such laws and codes build on, but are distinct from, the rules governing contracts in general.[40]

A first noteworthy point concerns concepts of *property* and ownership. Laws governing the sale of goods usually specify clearly the point at which the ownership interests in the goods sold pass from the seller to the buyer. This is important for several reasons. One reason relates to risk: the parties need to know when the risk of loss or damage passes from the seller to the buyer. In many commercial contracts—for example, a contract between a manufacturer and a buyer for the sale of two thousand motorcycles—the risk of loss or damage can be very large. Another reason for specifying the passage of ownership relates to financing a sale of goods. In some cases a buyer will not have adequate funds to pay for the goods directly and will instead need to obtain a loan from a bank. The bank typically will require that the buyer give the bank a security interest in the goods until the buyer has repaid the loan. If the buyer fails to repay the loan, the bank would be able to seize the goods. Because this amounts in effect to a splitting of property rights, the rules governing when and how such a security interest can be established are often complex. In fact, the Uniform Commercial Code adopted in

---

40. Among the most important international commercial codes are (i) the United Nations Convention on Contracts for the International Sale of Goods, discussed below and in Chapter IV, and (ii) the UNIDROIT Principles of International Commercial Contracts, described and reprinted in Michael Joachim Bonell, AN INTERNATIONAL RESTATEMENT OF CONTRACT LAW (Transnational Juris Publications, 1994).

most parts of the USA "recognizes six different property rights which can exist in the same goods at the same time: special property, insurable interest, title, risk of loss, right to possession, and security interest".[41]

A second special point about commercial contracts relates to the variety of *forms* that sales can take. The most straightforward sale would involve immediate exchange of the goods for the payment. Somewhat more complicated is the case in which delivery takes place in several installments, and payment is made on each installment. More complicated yet is the case in which delivery takes place in several installments but payment takes place on an entirely different schedule. Whenever these variations on the simple delivery-and-payment model appear, questions can arise about the respective rights and duties of the parties to the contract of sale, as well as the rights of third parties involved in the transaction (such as a bank providing a loan as mentioned in the preceding paragraph). Commercial laws are designed to answer those questions.

A third special point about commercial contracts relates to the *specific elements* that must be present in order for a sales contract to be properly formed and binding on the parties. The usual terms to be specified for such a contract, of course, would include (i) a description of the goods, (ii) the price, (iii) the quantity of goods sold, (iv) the time and place of delivery, and (v) the time and place and form of payment. But in a commercial setting, what if one or more of these are absent? While the rules vary somewhat from one legal system to another, a widely accepted approach (appearing in the United Nations Convention on Contracts for the International Sale of Goods, referred to below in section B of Chapter IV) is to consider a commercial contract to be complete (and therefore valid and enforceable) "if it indicates the goods and expressly or implicitly fixes or makes provisions for determining the quantity and price". In fact, a commercial contract might be complete even if it does not deal with price; unless the parties indicate otherwise, it can be assumed that they "impliedly made reference to the price generally charged at the time of

---

41. Cameron, *supra* note 1, at page 514.

the contract for such goods sold under comparable circumstances in the trade concerned".[42]

This approach, in which only a few of the usual elements actually need to be specified in order to create a binding commercial contract, reflects a basic assumption that has appeared in commercial law for several centuries, since the development of the *Lex Mercatoria* in Europe. That assumption is that commercial contracting behavior—that is, contracting for the sale of goods—is beneficial to all persons concerned and should be encouraged as much as possible. Modern commercial codes have typically been designed with that aim in mind—encouraging and supporting the sale of goods.

II.A.7. Electronic Commerce

The *physical* landscape of commercial activity is changing quickly. Now many businesses and individuals use computers and other electronic equipment to transmit messages, place orders, and conduct financial transactions, thus minimizing or even erasing some of the boundaries of space and time to which commerce has traditionally been subject. The term "electronic commerce" is used to refer to these dramatic changes.

The *legal* landscape of commercial activity—that is, the regime of laws and legal concepts developed over centuries to facilitate the sale of goods and services—is not changing as quickly. Indeed, although some changes have occurred in the legal landscape, it has not yet been altered adequately to accommodate the physical changes that have occurred. For example, many of the rules and principles of contract law described in the preceding sub-sections rest on the behavior of human beings who express their preferences and judgments to each other in order to form a contract. Do the same rules and principles work if applied not to human beings but to computers? Put differently, can com-

---

42. United Nations Convention on Contracts for the International Sale of Goods, opened for signature Apr. 11, 1980, entered into force Jan. 1, 1988, reprinted at 19 INTERNATIONAL LEGAL MATERIALS (1980), at page 668. The quoted language appears in Articles 14 and 55 of that treaty.

puters make contracts? In many automated businesses, computerized messages are transmitted to seek prices, place orders, and confirm orders—all without any human intervention or knowledge, except for having provided the initial programming for the computer programs. In such circumstances, our traditional views of contract law seem inadequate, because either (i) we need to take the position that computers have capacity to enter into contractual relationships—and perhaps that they are therefore to be treated as "legal persons"—or (ii) we need to stretch extremely far the concept of a "meeting of the [human] minds" (or "manifestation of assent") that usually signifies the existence of a contract between two contracting parties.

In addition to theoretical or conceptual difficulties posed by the recent development of electronic commerce, there are numerous practical difficulties in applying specific (traditional) rules of contract law to electronic commerce. Many nations, for example, require in their contract law or commercial code that certain types of contracts be "in writing" in order to be enforceable. Many times, however, electronic commerce is not documented in any physical document. Similarly, some nations require that certain contracts, to be legally enforceable, must be signed by the parties. Again, this might be an unwieldy or even impossible requirement to fulfill, especially with so much communication taking place by electronic mail or by direct transfer of information between computer systems.

Numerous efforts have been undertaken in recent years to accommodate the dramatic differences—specifically the conceptual, procedural, and physical differences—that exist between electronic commerce and more traditional commerce. Laws have recently been adopted in the USA, for example, to modify the "signed writing" requirements that date back to early English law and have appeared for many years in the Uniform Commercial Code.[43]

---

43. One such law is the Electronic Signatures in Global and National Commerce (E-SIGN) Act, enacted by the US Congress in 2000. At the state level, a uniform statute—the Uniform Electronic Transactions Act—was drafted in 1999 for state legislatures to enact. Certain changes have also been made to the Uniform Commercial Code. For several excerpts explaining legal developments in respect of electronic commerce, with specific attention paid to electronic "signatures", see Ralph H. Folsom, Michael W. Gordon, and John A. Spanogle, Jr.,

At the international level, UNCITRAL (the United Nations Commission on International Trade Law) approved in 1996 a "Model Law on Electronic Commerce", which nations can adopt in order to address a range of issues relating to electronic commerce. For example, that model law addresses questions of both writing requirements and signature requirements. In respect of the first of these, the model law provides that a nation's pre-existing legal rule calling for contracts to be in writing "is met by a data message if the information contained therein is accessible so as to be usable for subsequent reference".[44] In respect of signature requirements, the model law provides that such a requirement will be met by a data message if there are adequate and reliable methods to identify the person sending the message "and to indicate that person's approval of the information contained in the data message".[45]

In addition to this UNCITRAL initiative, the International Chamber of Commerce ("ICC") also has promulgated a set of legal principles for digital signatures, known as the General Usage for International Digitally Ensured Commerce (GUIDEC). The GUIDEC effort may be regarded as an improvement on the UNCITRAL model law because it provides more detail, particularly in developing a standard vocabulary for dealing with electronic signatures and thereby goes "a long way toward developing that legitimacy that is so important for the future of electronic commerce generally."[46] More recently yet, a treaty emerging from UNCITRAL's efforts—the 2005 United Nations

---

INTERNATIONAL BUSINESS TRANSACTIONS (West Publishing, Fifth Edition, 2002), at pages 170–184. See also see Gaylord A. Jentz, Roger Le Roy Miller, and Frank B. Cross, WEST'S BUSINESS LAW (West Educational Publishing, 1999), at pages 224–226.

44. UNCITRAL Model Law on Electronic Commerce (1996), at Article 6. The term "data message" is defined to include information transmitted by electronic mail, electronic data interchange (EDI), telegram, telex, or telecopy. *Id.* at Article 2(a). For the UNCITRAL Model Law and other UNCITRAL efforts in this area, see www.uncitral.org.

45. UNCITRAL Model Law on Electronic Commerce (1996), at Article 7.

46. William F. Fox, Jr., *The International Chamber of Commerce's GUIDEC Principles: Private-Sector Rules for Digital Signatures*, 35 THE INTERNATIONAL LAWYER 71 (2001). The same issue of THE INTERNATIONAL LAWYER (Spring 2001) includes several other articles emerging from a "Symposium on Borderless Elec-

Convention on the Use of Electronic Communications in International Contracts—is designed to enhance legal certainty and commercial predictability in cases where electronic communications are used in international transactions. So far, that treaty has relatively few parties (less than a dozen as of mid-2007).

Further Readings on Contracts

(in addition to the sources cited in footnotes in this section)

Contracts (Third Edition, 1999), by E. Allan Farnsworth

Drafting Contracts (Second Edition, 1993), by Scott J. Burnham

Murray on Contracts (Fourth Edition, 2001), by John Edward Murray, Jr.

An Introduction to The Law of Contract (Fifth Edition, 1995), by P.S. Atiyah

Foundations of Contract Law (1994), collection edited by Richard Craswell and Alan Schwartz

Contract Law in The Netherlands (1995), by A.S. Hartkamp

Contract Law and Practice: The English System and Continental Comparisons (Fourth Edition, 2001), by Michael H. Whincup

Black Letter on Contracts (Second Edition, 1990), by the late John D. Calamari and Joseph M. Perillo

Contracts (1999), by the same authors

Contracts in a Nutshell (Fourth Edition, 1997), by Gordon D. Schaber and Claude D. Rohwer

The Law of Contract (1993), by Sir J. Smith

Remedies for Breach of Contract—A Comparative Account (1991), by G. H. Treitel

Davies on Contract (Eighth Edition, 1999), by R. Upex

International Encyclopedia of Laws—Contracts (1996 Edition), edited by Jacques H. Herbots

---

tronic Commerce". For details about work within the OECD on electronic commerce, see www.oecd.org.

An International Restatement of Contract Law — The UNIDROIT Principles of International Commercial Contracts (Second Edition, 1997), by Michael Joachim Bonell

Sale of Goods (Ninth Edition, 2001), by P.S. Atiyah

Uniform Commercial Code — Terms and Transactions in Commercial Law (1991), by John F. Dolan

Uniform Commercial Code (2002), by James J. White and Robert S. Summers

II.B. Resolution of Commercial Disputes

The preceding paragraphs enumerated several key provisions that need to be included in commercial sales contracts. Some commercial laws require that these provisions be specified in order for the contract to be enforceable. Not required, but often just as important, is another type of provision — the provision governing the resolution of disputes that might arise under the contract.

Dispute resolution provisions are especially important in international commercial contracts — that is, contracts for the sale of goods across national borders. Such transactions have, of course, been undertaken for many centuries. Indeed, those transactions gave birth to a system of international commercial arbitration that originated in medieval Western Europe during the growth of the mercantile trade between nation-states. Disputes then were arbitrated "within communities consisting either of participants in an individual trade or of persons enrolled in bodies established under the auspices and control of geographical trading centres".[47]

The rationales for commercial dispute resolution have remained the same throughout the centuries. The reasons include these: (i) to handle disagreements between parties, preferably in a less formal and

---

47. Alan Redfern et al., LAW AND PRACTICE OF INTERNATIONAL COMMERCIAL ARBITRATION (4th ed. 2004), at page 2 (quoting from a 2004 work by Michael Mustill).

(sometimes) less expensive way than that provided by applicable rules and procedures used in courts of law[48]; (ii) to choose a neutral forum and tribunal, as will be discussed in more detail below; (iii) to obtain a ruling against the losing party that can be enforced both nationally and internationally, under local laws where the arbitration takes place and under treaty provisions, such as those of the New York Convention (discussed later); and (iv) to provide a large measure of flexibility and confidentiality to the proceedings.[49] Dispute resolution situations at the international level, and how to deal with them, are summarized in Chapter IV of this book. Even in domestic sales transactions, however, it is important to consider the subject of dispute resolution, preferably before a dispute arises.

II.B.1. Choices of Law, Forum, and Procedures

Three closely related topics bear on dispute resolution and on the drafting of appropriate contractual provisions. The first is *choice of law*. The general trend internationally is to permit parties to a contract a wide degree of freedom in choosing the set of legal rules that will govern their contractual relation. A few countries still require that contracts entered into within their territories must be governed by domestic (local) law. In most cases, however, the parties can select other rules. This is especially important if one party to a contract entered into within the territory of one country is from another country, or if the subject-matter of the sales transaction is one in which another country's law is more fully developed than the "home" country's law.

The second related topic is *choice of forum*. This refers to the court or other adjudicative body to which any dispute is to be submitted. Again, domestic sales contracts usually require no specific designation of the forum, unless perhaps the two parties are located in different parts of the country and wish to specify in advance (and are

---

48. *Id.*
49. See *id.* at pages 22–23.

permitted under court rules to so specify) which particular court should hear any dispute that arises later between them.

The third related topic concerns *alternative dispute resolution*. In most countries, the parties may choose to handle disputes through commercial arbitration or other means of dispute resolution that are less formal and less public than the court system usually is. The full range of alternative dispute resolution procedures available in sales contracts includes the following (and variations on each): (i) commercial arbitration; (ii) conciliation; (iii) mediation; and (iv) negotiation. These terms and concepts differ, of course, from one country and language to the next. Here is one commonly-accepted set of definitions of these four approaches:

Arbitration   a procedure that is similar to public, formal litigation (through the state-supplied court system) but that is handled largely outside that system and that therefore is subject to much greater input by the parties as to the identity of the arbitrators, the rules those arbitrators should use in determining the rights and responsibilities of the parties, the procedures (including time limits) that the arbitrators should follow in coming to a decision and announcing it, and the language and location of the arbitral proceedings.

Conciliation   a procedure that is more informal than either arbitration or litigation and that involves a person (a conciliator) who reviews the claims of both the parties to a dispute and offers solutions that will not focus principally on the allocation of blame but instead on the repair of the damage that the dispute has caused or threatens to the business relationship between the parties.

Mediation   a "go-between" procedure in which a person (a mediator) acts as a vehicle for communications between the parties, so that their differing views on the dispute can be understood and perhaps reconciled, but with the primary responsibility for arriving at such a reconciliation still resting on the parties themselves as opposed to any intermediary person.

Negotiation   direct discussions between the parties, without involvement of a mediator, conciliator, arbitrator, or any
other outside persons—with the hope that the business decision-makers can resolve the dispute without
any formal or external proceedings.

Many commercial contracts incorporate dispute-resolution provisions that include more than one of the options described above. For
example, such a provision might require that in the case of a dispute
arising out of the contractual relationship, the parties will first attempt to resolve it through negotiation or mediation; and that if that
attempt fails the parties will submit the dispute to arbitration following a specified procedure. That procedure often provides that each
of the two parties to the contract will appoint one arbitrator and that
those two arbitrators will select a third arbitrator, who will serve as
chairman of the arbitral panel.

II.B.2. Focus on Commercial Arbitration

It is important to identify some of the *key reasons* why arbitration
in particular has gained favor in recent years, especially in international
commercial dealings but also in purely domestic transactions. First, in
many cases arbitration can be started more promptly and completed
more quickly than litigation, especially where courts are plagued with
more cases than they can possibly handle. Second, arbitration usually
involves arbitrators who have some expertise in the subject-matter of
the dispute they are hearing. For example, two parties to a commercial contract (the sale of goods by a producer to a wholesaler, for instance) may include in their sales contract an arbitration clause under
which the arbitrators (if needed) would have experience in the economic sector at issue. Third, arbitration affords neutrality. This is particularly important in situations (for example, cross-border transactions) in which there is a perceived risk that a court would tend to be
biased in favor of one of the parties to a dispute. Fourth, courts are increasingly agreeable to enforcing the judgments of arbitral tribunals.

This last point warrants special attention. Modern arbitration
laws typically ensure the effectiveness of commercial arbitration pro-

cedures as an alternative form of dispute resolution by providing that local courts: (i) should honor the intention of the parties to a commercial transaction to designate arbitration rather than litigation as the method for settling disputes (that is, the courts should enforce the agreement to arbitrate); (ii) should, more specifically, also honor the intention of the parties to prescribe whatever specific rules they want regarding the conduct of the arbitration, including the rules of procedure, the substantive rules, the place of arbitration, and so forth; (iii) should assist the arbitrators with the gathering of any evidence the arbitrators consider necessary; (iv) should not undertake an independent assessment of the arbitrators' decision; and (v) should enforce any interim order or final award made by the arbitrators.

A final matter should be noted regarding commercial arbitration: there is an important distinction between (i) the inclusion of an arbitration provision in a contract (or perhaps in a separate arbitration agreement) *before* any dispute arises between the parties and (ii) the attempt to conclude an arbitration agreement *after* a dispute arises. As may perhaps be self-evident, the first of these approaches is typically much more effective, because (as noted in the preceding paragraph) courts typically will give effect to such an arbitration provision, thereby cutting off the possibility that one of the contracting parties will be able to initiate litigation. If the parties wait until *after* a dispute arises, the likelihood of reaching an agreement to handle the dispute through arbitration declines substantially.

Further information about commercial arbitration, especially in the context of international sales contracts, appears in Chapter IV of this book.

Further Readings on Resolution of Commercial Disputes

(in addition to the sources cited in footnotes in this section)

International Handbook on Commercial Arbitration: National Reports and Basic Legal Texts (1998), edited by Pieter Sanders and Albert Jan van den Berg

Law and Practice of International Commercial Arbtitration (Fourth Edition, 2004), by Alan Redfern and Martin Hunter

The Internationalization of International Arbitration (1995), by V.V. Veeder, Martin Hunter, and Arthur Marriott

Arbitration Law and Procedure (1994), by Michael Forde

Alternative Dispute Resolution (1992), by A. Bevan

II.C. Banking Law

Early banking was first provided by merchants, money changers, goldsmiths, and nobles, who took deposits from other individuals for safekeeping and convenience. The holders of the deposits frequently paid interest to the individuals but then lent out the deposits at higher interest rates to borrowers, thereby making a profit and, in effect, increasing the supply of "money" (through the credit that those loans represented) in the economic system of the region where they operated. Banking activities of this sort greatly enlarged the financial potential of cities, states, republics, kingdoms, and empires through history because they could (through their leaders) build more roads, ships, armies, and so forth. However, because risk was inherent in private banking, many countries created national banks to achieve stronger, more reliable banking activity and to impose more centralized control over some aspects of the operations of the private banks.[50]

Thus were born the two basic levels or "tiers" of financial institutions in a national banking system: (i) the central bank and (ii) commercial banks. This "two-tier" banking system exists in nearly all countries now; the single-tier or "monobank" system largely disappeared with the dissolution of the Soviet Union.

Banking law in most countries reflects this two-tier structure. That is, banking law is usually divided into two principal sets of rules—those governing the central bank and those governing commercial banks. Specialized banks exist in many countries and these sometimes operate under a third set of rules. Generally speaking, the trend in recent years

---

50. See William A. Lovett, BANKING AND FINANCIAL INSTITUTIONS LAW (6th ed. 2005), at pages 3–5.

has been away from the application of a separate set of rules for such specialized banks (for example, development banks and savings banks).

II.C.1. The Central Bank

Although business entities have little direct involvement with the operations of the central bank, that institution plays a pivotal role in the economic life of the nation. The central bank serves several *key functions*. Although these vary somewhat from country to country and are sometimes shared with an agency more closely associated with the political and bureaucratic agencies of government (usually the Ministry of Finance), the functions usually include the following:

- to promote and maintain price stability;
- to issue currency;
- to act as agent, banker, and advisor to the government;
- to act as lender of last resort to commercial banks;
- to engage in commercial bank supervision; and
- to hold and manage the country's foreign exchange reserves.

Of these functions, the first one is widely regarded as the most important. *Price stability* means principally that the purchasing power of the national currency is maintained over time. It does not, of course, mean the fixing of prices for individual goods or services. Such individual prices are established by the interplay of supply and demand within the economy. But the overall strength of the national currency as measured against a basic package of such goods and services must be maintained from one year to the next in order for any economy to function well and fairly. It is that goal that is usually foremost for a central bank. In order to achieve it, the central banking laws usually authorize the central bank to employ several "instruments of monetary policy". These typically include (i) the making of loans to commercial banks (and, within certain limits, to the government), (ii) the setting of interest rates on such loans, (iii) the setting of reserve requirements (amounts of funds that commercial banks must set aside or must place on deposit with the central bank), (iv) the purchase and sale of government securities in "open market

operations", and (v) the issuance of central bank securities (debt instruments in the name of the central bank itself), along with certain
other methods of influencing the supply of money in the economy.
The effectiveness of a central bank in achieving the aim of price stability, and in carrying out its other functions, depends on several factors. Key among these factors are (i) the competence and honesty of
the central bank's management and (ii) the autonomy of the central
bank—that is, its independence from political pressures that often
come from government officials with short-term interests. In order to
assure such autonomy, central bank laws usually include provisions
establishing a separate financial foundation for the central bank, long
terms for the governor and directors of the bank, and rules disallow-
ing their dismissal except in extraordinary circumstances.

II.C.2. Commercial Banks and Specialized Banks

Commercial banks serve as important engines of economic activity in a country, converting the fuel of individual savings into the energy of business financing. They are intermediaries. A common *definition of the term "bank"* reflects this role: "an entity engaged in the
business of (i) taking deposits and paying on drafts written by its customers, and (ii) making loans for its own account".[51] (In some countries there may be several types of financial institutions that meet this
definition even though they carry labels or titles other than "bank";
for our purposes here, any such institution will be considered a bank
if it meets the two-part definition.)

Stated in concrete terms, a bank carries out *two basic functions*.
First, it accepts money from customers who wish to place their funds
on deposit for safekeeping; usually the bank pays interest on those deposits, or certain types of them. Second, with the funds thus received

---

51. For a survey of definitions of "bank" and "banking business" in various
countries, see Wernhard Möschel, *Public Law of Banking*, in INTERNATIONAL EN-
CYCLOPEDIA OF COMPARATIVE LAW (Vol. IX, Ch. 3), at pages 43–48 (Oceana
Publications, 1991). Some of the contents of this section, and especially the
"Other Issues" in subsection 3 below, are drawn from that publication.

from depositors, the bank makes loans to business entities and individuals. On the assumption that only a small proportion of the depositors will want to withdraw their funds at any one point in time, the bank lends out most of the funds deposited with it.

A major risk of such operations, of course, is that the bank will lend out so large a proportion of the funds on deposit that the bank will be unable to service depositors wanting to make withdrawals. If that happens, or if depositors fear that it might happen, a "run" can take place in which many depositors demand their funds at one time. That, in turn can cause havoc in the entire financial system and the nation's economy, since failure of one bank can undercut the confidence that depositors and customers have in other banks. (This has happened many times in many countries, including in the USA during the 1980s' "savings-and-loan crisis".) Because the financial system depends largely on confidence—including confidence that government regulation of banks will be effective to guard against fraud or incompetence in their operations—the central bank (or other supervisor of commercial banks) has an important role in a country's economic stability.

It is for this reason that much of the banking law in any country revolves around ensuring the *safety and prudence* of banks. That overall goal of prudential regulation has been explained by one authority as comprising three distinct but related objectives:

- to sustain systemic stability—that is, limiting the risk that the entire financial system in a country (or a region) will collapse;
- to maintain the safety and soundness of particular institutions within the overall financial system—that is, limiting the risk that the peculiar circumstances of an individual bank will lead it to fail; and
- to protect the consumer—that is, requiring banks to follow certain rules in their treatment of customers, and especially their depositors.[52]

---

52. Klaas Knot, *Banking Supervision at the Crossroads: Background and Overview*, appearing as chapter 1 in BANKING SUPERVISION AT THE CROSSROADS (Thea Kuppens et al, eds. 2003), at page 5.

It is against the backdrop of those objectives that a country's banking law will, for example, typically include provisions that:

- prohibit any person from engaging in banking business without a license;
- authorize the central bank (which is in many countries entrusted with bank supervision duties) to scrutinize an application for a banking license in order to guard against unqualified managers or inadequate capitalization;
- require banks to submit periodic reports to the central bank and to cooperate with central bank inspections—both "on-site" and "off-site" inspections—of bank operations;
- prescribe minimum amounts of capitalization and liquidity;
- place limits on the amount of lending a bank can do in favor of a single borrower, so as to avoid dangerous concentration of the risk of default;
- place other limits on the types of transactions banks can engage in (for example, a bank usually cannot invest in land or take an equity position in a manufacturing company), so that depositors and creditors are protected against imprudent decisions or fraudulent actions by the bank; and
- permit the central bank to take enforcement actions against a bank that fails to meet its obligations, including the authority of the central bank to take over a bank's operations temporarily in extraordinary circumstances and, if necessary, to liquidate or restructure the bank (see also the reference to "handling insolvent banks" under "Other Issues" in subsection 3, below).

Despite the strong supervisory powers that the central bank is typically given over the commercial banks in an economy, the fact remains—and the law usually ensures—that banks are fully responsible for making their own lending decisions. Most countries have now rejected the system in which banks were primarily involved in making "directed credits"—that is, loans to particular businesses as directed by the government or the central bank. Instead, commercial banks are to appraise loan applications purely on the basis of the creditworthiness of the person or entity seeking the loan.

Exceptions to these general rules apply where "*specialized banks*" are involved. For example, development banks are established to make loans that will serve the economic development interests of the country. Where such specialized banks do exist, a balance must be struck, and is usually required by law, between (i) the need to direct credit to particular economic sectors (for example, the agriculture sector or a specified geographic area) against (ii) the need to permit resources to be applied to creditworthy purposes that are proven efficient by the rules of supply and demand.

II.C.3. Other Issues in Banking and Monetary Law

Over the last several decades, *multinational banking* has become more important as deposit, loan, financing, securities transactions, and currency exchange activities became more globalized. Just in the past dozen years or so, numerous "mega-mergers" occurred among multinational banks, investment bankers, and major insurance companies in the USA, Europe, and Japan. Interestingly, however, as of April 2004, only one US multinational bank, Citigroup, managed to rank in the top ten multinational banks around the world, while the United Kingdom, France, and Japan each had two. Many controversies and issues have emerged with the introduction and growth of multinational banks, such as (i) alleged tax avoidance by many such banks, (ii) inadequate reserves held by such banks as protection against big risks, and (iii) inappropriate lending to governments of countries that are saddled with political risks or that engage in excessive borrowing and pose dangers of default.[53]

Other issues deserve mention in this respect as well. One is *deposit insurance*. In many countries, a system of insurance or guarantee has been established, either with government funds or through cooperative arrangements among the banks themselves. These systems, which date back in some form to the early 1800s in the USA and India but

---

53. See Lovett, *supra* note 50, at pages 218–219, 228.

were put in place in the 1970s in most countries, are designed to provide a guarantee to depositors that their deposits, up to a prescribed amount, will be available to them even if the bank at issue becomes insolvent (unable to pay its obligations, including its obligations to depositors). In many cases the legal provisions governing such a system appear in a separate law.

Also appearing in separate laws, or in a criminal code, are provisions regarding *counterfeiting* of currency and mutilation of coins and banknotes. Related to these are rules on the return of old currency for new currency when a change in currency is necessary (often because of political circumstances, such as a merger of two countries or division of a country).

Several of the prudential standards applicable to commercial banks have now been addressed in *international regulations.* These include, for example, rules on capital adequacy established in 1988 by the Basle Committee on International Convergence of Capital Measurement and Capital Standards. Those Basle capital-adequacy rules are very well known by most bank managers and regulators around the world, although the rules are often not followed. The fundamental concept of the rules is that a bank needs to maintain a prescribed ratio of capital (especially owner equity) to "risk-based assets"—that is, the amounts of loans that are owed to the bank, as discounted to reflect the risk that those loans will not be repaid.

Many countries have now accepted various guidelines established by the Basle committee on capital standards, as well as various guidelines prescribed by another committee—the Basle Committee on Banking Supervision. Both of these committees consist of officials that are drawn from the member states of the Group of Ten countries and that deal with issues of common concern as banking business becomes more global in scope and effect. Within the context of Europe, banking regulation is the subject of extensive EU legislation designed to respond to the rapid transformation from numerous national financial markets into a single integrated EU wide financial market.[54]

---

54. For a wide-ranging discussion of trends in international financial supervision, especially in Europe, see the collection of essays in BANKING SUPERVISION AT THE CROSSROADS, *supra* note 52.

A topic of banking law that has attracted particular interest following the Asian financial crisis that began in 1997 is that of *handling insolvent banks*. Modern practice[55] insists that there should be a clear and detailed legal framework that authorizes competent and independent government officials (i) to identify, on objective grounds, when a bank has become, or is about to become, insolvent (either by "book insolvency" or "liquidity-based insolvency"), (ii) to take prompt action (including, in some cases, a takeover of the control of the bank) to protect the interests of depositors and other creditors of the bank, in order to prevent a crisis of confidence in the financial system generally, and (iii) to provide, where appropriate, for the "exit" of the bank from the financial system through liquidation, merger, or some other form of reorganization.

Recent attention has focused also on *money laundering*. The process of money laundering has been described in this way:

> Money laundering begins with dirty money. Money can get dirty in two ways. One way is through tax evasion; people make money legally, but they make more money than they report to the government. Money also gets dirty through illegal generation. Common techniques include drug sales, gambling, and bribery. Once money is dirty, it must converted into an apparently legitimate form, or "laundered" before it can be invested or spent.[56]

---

55. For a discussion of bank insolvency, and methods for avoiding and responding to it, see Robert Lee Ramsey and John W. Head, Preventing Financial Chaos: An International Guide to Legal Rules and Operational Procedures for Handling Insolvent Banks (Kluwer Law International 2000).

56. Norman Abrams and Sara Sun Beale, Federal Criminal Law and Its Enforcement (West Publishing, 3d ed., 2000), at page 385 (quoting from Sarah N. Welling, *Smurfs, Money Laundering, and the Federal Criminal Law: The Crime of Structuring Transactions*, 41 Florida Law Review (1989), at pages 287, 290–292). See also Sarah N. Welling, Sara Sun Beale, and Pamela H. Bucy, Federal Criminal Law and Related Actions, vol. 2 (West Publishing, 1998), at Chapter 18 (pages 75–157), and in particular the bibliography at page 157. Much of the content of these paragraphs on money laundering draws from the texts cited above.

Money laundering, then, is the process by which someone conceals the existence, illegal source, or illegal application of income, and then disguises that income to make it appear legitimate. Money laundering is harmful because (among other reasons) it allows the underlying criminal activity to thrive. Such criminal activity often consists of drug sales and gambling.

How do governments combat money laundering? One of the key methods is by imposing reporting requirements on banks, so that unusually large or suspicious transactions are reported to bank regulatory agencies, and then making the failure to abide by those reporting requirements a serious crime that can attract heavy penalties for a noncomplying bank or its officers. Another method of combating money laundering is to require that any person transporting large amounts of cash into or out of a country report that fact to government authorities. Yet another method is to require banks to freeze any accounts that they determine to be held by certain designated terrorist organizations. [57]

Besides banks, there are in most economies a variety of other entities, so-called *non-bank financial institutions*, that carry out some functions of banks but do not meet both elements of the definition of a "bank" as explained above (taking deposits and making loans). These non-bank financial institutions include development finance companies, investment companies, insurance companies, pension funds, housing finance companies, pawnshops, and other entities having various names and features. In most countries, responsibility for regulating the operations of these non-bank financial institutions is not placed with the central bank but instead with other government agencies.

Although both sides of commercial bank operations—deposit-taking and lending—usually involve the payment of interest, this is not the usual practice in traditional *Islamic banking law*. Instead, a variety of alternative arrangements have been put in place. For example, depositors may be placed in a position equivalent to those of joint venturers in the investments that their banks finance.[58] Why would

---

57. For a discussion of these methods of dealing with money laundering, see subsection E.2. of Chapter III, below.

58. Numerous texts are now available on Islamic banking law. For an excellent collection of essays not only on that subject but on Islamic commercial law

this be the case? Because of the principles on which Islamic banking rest. One authority has summarized those principles in this way:

> *Principles of an Islamic financial system.* The basic framework for an Islamic financial system is a set of rules and laws, collectively referred to as *shariah*, governing economic, social, political, and cultural aspects of Islamic societies. *Shariah* originates from the rules dictated by the *Quran* and its practices, and explanations rendered (more comonly known as *Sunnah*) by the Prophet Muhammad [*PBUH*]. Further elaboration of the rules is provided by scholars in Islamic jurisprudence within the framework of the *Quran* and *Sunnah*. The basic principles of an Islamic financial system can be summarized as follows:
>
> *Prohibition of interest.* Prohibition of *riba*, a term literally meaning "an excess" and interpreted as "any unjustifiable increase of capital whether in loans or sales" is the central tenet of the system. More precisely, any positive, fixed, predetermined rate tied to the maturity and the amount of principal (i.e., guaranteed regardless of the performance of the investment) is considered *riba* and is prohibited. The general consensus among Islamic scholars is that *riba* covers not only usury [excessive interest] but also the charging of "interest" as widely practiced....
>
> *Risk sharing.* Because interest is prohibited, suppliers of funds become investors instead of creditors. The provider of financial capital and the entrepreneur share business risks in return for shares of the profits....
>
> *Prohibition of speculative behavior.* An Islamic financial system discourages hoarding and prohibits transactions featuring extreme uncertainties, gambling, and risks.
>
> *Sanctity of contracts.* Islam upholds contractual obligations and the disclosure of information as a sacred duty.

---

more generally—in the specific context of the region referred to in the West as the Middle East—see ARAB COMMERCIAL LAW (William M. Ballantyne & Howard L. Stovall, eds., 2002).

Shariah-approved activities. Only those business activities that do not violate the rules of *shariah* qualify for investment. For example, any investment in businesses dealing with alcohol, gambling, and casinos would be prohibited.[59]

A last topic in this brief survey of issues relating to banks and banking operations is that of **payments systems.** A payments system, at its most basic level, is an agreed-upon way to transfer value between a buyer and a seller in a transaction.[60] In less economically developed countries, the predominant way of transferring value is by using currency (money) or by barter (exchange of commodities); in more economically developed countries, more sophisticated methods of transferring value are used — that is, not only currency but also checks and electronic transfers. Most countries have established more or less detailed rules for managing the transfer of value, as well as for so-called "clearing and settlement" functions. These relate, for example, to the process by which a check written by a Buyer is given to a Seller, deposited into the Seller's bank, sorted, presented by that bank to the Buyer's bank, and collected against by the Buyer's bank to the Seller's bank. The rules established by a country to govern such transactions (and established more recently between countries for this purpose) are related, of course, to those governing "commercial paper" as discussed above in subsection C.3. of Chapter I.

Further Readings on Banking Law

(in addition to the sources cited in endnotes for this section)

Public Law of Banking (1991), by Wernhard Möschel

Modern Banking Law (Third Edition, 2002), by E.P. Ellinger, Eva Lomnicka, and Richard Hodey

The Law and Regulation of Financial Institutions (Second Edition, 1998), by Milton R. Schroeder

---

59. Zamir Iqbal, *Islamic Financial Systems*, appearing in Finance and Development (June 1997), at page 43.
60. David B. Humphrey, *Payment Systems: Principles, Practice, and Improvements*, appearing as World Bank Technical Paper Number 260 (1995), at page 3.

Banking Laws and Regulations—An Economic Perspective (1987), by Nicholas A. Lash

Law of Banking (Fourth Edition, 1992), by Ian F. G. Baxter

Devising International Bank Supervisory Standards (1995), by Joseph J. Norton

Encyclopedia of Banking and Finance (Ninth Edition, 1993), by Glenn Munn, F.L. Garcia, and others

Money and Banking (Tenth Edition, 1992), by David R. Kamerschen

II.D. Insurance

For an economy to be vibrant, business entities must have some confidence that they can succeed—not necessarily that they surely *will* succeed, but at least that the conditions for success are favorable. In order for someone engaged in business to have that necessary confidence, there must be some way of **controlling various types of risk**. To some degree, of course, business entities control risk by adhering to age-old practices of cautious management, honest dealing, and hard work. Some risks, however, are largely beyond the control of a businessperson. These include the risk of fire, the risk of theft, the risk of accidental loss or damage, the risk of fraud committed by other people, and so forth. Any of these eventualities, if they occur, can spell disaster for a business. Accordingly, a businessperson typically will want to transfer these risks to someone else. A primary way of doing that is through insurance, under which the risk shouldered by a particular business entity can be reduced dramatically by sharing it with many other entities.

The business of insurance has a long history. Like most business developments, the first forms of insurance protection evolved to promote inter-regional trading and shipping. Contracts designed to pool the risks faced by caravans and shipping can be traced back to ancient Mesopotamia. Medieval Italian merchants created modern insurance business practice when they began to provide marine risk coverage (that is, contracts by which one company promises to a sizeable group of shipping companies that it will pay for specified unforeseen losses suffered by any one of them). Later, in the late 17th century when Great Britain began to dominate marine commerce, Lloyd's Coffee House in London became a convenient headquarters for such contracts to be struck between underwriters and merchants (see below for details of how this worked). In the 18th century, British and other European businesses developed simple fire and life insurance contracts.[61]

II.D.1. Key Elements of Insurance

One author has defined an insurance contract as having three key elements: (1) the distribution of risk, (2) among a substantial number of members, (3) through a person or entity engaged primarily in the business of insurance.[62] The following discussion of insurance elaborates on those three elements.

In any economic system, it is possible to envision a variety of ways in which society might decide to allocate the economic loss that results from any misfortune. Assume that the misfortune is the destruction of a manufacturing plant by fire. The economic loss caused by the fire could be suffered by the owner of the manufacturing plant. Alternatively, it could be borne by any person who caused the fire, whether deliberately or through negligence, assuming such a person could be found. Perhaps some sharing of the economic loss could take place between those two parties.

Under a system of insurance, the economic loss is *distributed* among many persons—in fact, among as many as possible of those persons who are subject to the same kind of risk. The typical arrangement is for each such person (either natural person or business entity) to pay into a general fund a standardized amount of money, usually called a "premium", and for each person who actually experiences the misfortune to be paid from that fund in the amount of that economic loss (or some smaller amount agreed on in advance). Of

---

61. See Lovett, *supra* note 50, at pages 352–354, 362.

62. John F. Dobbyn, INSURANCE LAW IN A NUTSHELL (West Publishing, 2nd edition, 1989), at pages 1–2. The following paragraphs draw from that and other sources.

course, no person subject to such an arrangement can know in advance whether he or she will, over any particular period, realize a net "gain" or a net "loss" from participating in it—that is, no insured person will know in advance whether he or she will pay more into the fund or receive more out of it. The appeal of participating in the arrangement, however, is that it reduces the risk of financial loss to a measurable and acceptable level for all insured persons. Instead of being exposed to a small risk that a financially disastrous misfortune will occur, the insured person now is exposed to a relatively small and known cost and to no risk at all (except for the risk that the insurance arrangement will fail, as discussed below).

In order for such an arrangement to work effectively, and to be considered insurance, it must involve a relatively *large number of persons* among which the risk is spread. Typically, the greater the number of persons among whom the risk is spread, the smaller will be the amount each insured person will need to pay in the form of a premium. As a practical matter, most effective insurance arrangements involve hundreds or thousands of insured persons. In the case of an insured business entity, a further amount of risk spreading often occurs because the business entity will typically pass along the costs of the insurance premiums to its customers in the form of slightly higher fees for services or costs for goods sold by the business entity.

There are many different types of arrangements in which costs are spread among a large number of people. If, for example, a company selling telephones offers a pre-paid repair service, the cost incurred by the company in carrying out a few repairs on those telephones that need repair will be spread over many purchasers, so that the price charged to any one customer for the pre-paid repair service is relatively small. In that case, however, there is not an insurance contract, according to the usual definition as offered above, because the risk-distribution is not handled by *a company primarily in the business of insurance.* For the telephone manufacturing company, repair services are only incidental to its overall business operations. By contrast, an insurance company has as its main business (i) the collection of premiums from a large number of people expressly for the purpose of spreading the risk, (ii) the investigation of claims and payment of the legitimate ones, and (iii) the prudent financial management of the funds in its possession.

Theoretically, it would not be necessary for the insurance company to hold funds—that is, to collect premium payments in advance. It could instead enter into contracts with persons who commit to make payments if and when legitimate claims are made. This type of structure, which was used early in the development of insurance law, has been discarded because of its impracticality. Therefore insurance companies today are repositories of very large amounts of money. Government regulation of insurance companies includes, among other things, stringent requirements about the prudent and conservative handling and investment of such funds.

II.D.2. Types of Insurance; Insurable Interests

There is no theoretical limitation to the types of risks that could be insured against. As a practical matter, however, the types of risk that business entities can get insurance for are confined mainly to the following: (i) fire and casualty insurance and (ii) marine and "inland marine" insurance. Both terms have considerably wider applicability than the words themselves would suggest.

Combined *fire and casualty* insurance provides comprehensive coverage on real property (land and buildings) and on many other types of business property. Fire insurance obviously covers loss caused by fire—or at least by fire that is not deliberately started or fueled by the insured person. Fire insurance also usually covers losses caused by lightning or by explosion, as well as losses caused by other natural disasters that have nothing to do with fire: earthquake, water, wind, rain, collision, and riot. Casualty insurance widens the scope of coverage to include other types of losses, including those caused by theft, machinery breakdown, unusual costs arising from injuries to workers, and other business-related losses. (It is worth noting that in many cases flood insurance is handled separately from general fire and casualty insurance—a fact that many people discover to their despair after suffering the damaging effects of a flood.)

Marine insurance covers ships and their cargo against loss or damage at sea. The history of marine insurance is described by one writer as follows:

The current pattern of marine insurance is a direct descendant of the custom that developed in the 1600's at the Lloyd's Coffee House in London. A shipper or shipowner interested in insuring a vessel cargo would pass around a slip of paper among those gathered indicating the relevant facts and the amount of insurance sought. Anyone interested would write on the slip the amount of insurance that he would offer, the rate, and his initials. These latter became known as 'underwriters.' The major difference today is that most underwriting is done by corporations rather than individuals.[63]

As the term "*inland marine insurance*" suggests, such coverage extends to losses occurring during transportation other than on the high seas. It is not, however, confined to inland transportation only by water. Instead, it covers goods being moved by other forms of transportation, and even certain types of goods that are not being moved at all but that are not the kind of fixtures for which fire and casualty insurance is designed. Indeed, a type of insurance policy that goes by the odd name of "business floater policy" can be used to provide coverage against nearly all types of risk to a business entity's equipment and inventory.

In order for a person or business entity to obtain insurance coverage of any of the types described above, it will be necessary for that person or entity to show an "*insurable interest*". This requirement arose long ago to guard against fraud: if a person having no ownership interest in a ship, for example, were permitted to purchase an insurance policy covering the loss of that ship at sea, that person might intentionally have the ship destroyed in order to collect the benefit payment, and would not have suffered any real loss with the destruction of the ship. Although that logical basis for the requirement of an insurable interest is fairly straightforward, the requirement is sometimes not easy to apply. Insurance laws typically specify in some detail what type of "interest"—full legal ownership, shared ownership, a creditor's interest, possible future own-

---

63. *Id.* at page 27.

ership, or other interest—is adequate to permit a person to obtain insurance.

II.D.3. Other Insurance Issues

Other matters that are covered by insurance laws typically include some or all of the following:

- *public policy exceptions*—circumstances in which insurance contracts cannot be entered into because of some kind of illegality or inappropriateness. For example, in some countries it is impossible to obtain insurance against damage to gambling equipment or against loss of inventory of a business entity that is operating without a proper license.
- *intentional conduct exception*—the doctrine that insurance coverage does not extend to a loss deliberately caused through the actions (or inaction) by the insured person. The example given above related to fire: if the insured person sets fire to his own office building, he usually cannot collect on the insurance policy covering that building.
- *indemnity insurance*—coverage that protects an insured against legal liability to a third party. For example, a business entity might obtain indemnity insurance to guard against large losses that might result if a customer were to bring a lawsuit for physical injury suffered by that customer while she was on the business entity's premises or using the business entity's products.
- *procedures for filing claims*—insurance contracts usually specify in detail the obligation of the insured to notify the insurance company immediately of the loss, to prove in detail the type and extent of the loss, to bring a claim within a certain period of time after the claim arose, and to cooperate with the insurance company in investigating and defending against any action brought by third parties.
- *defenses of the insurer*—grounds on which the insurance company can legally refuse to pay the benefits claimed by the insured party. Such refusal is possible, for example, if the insured

party concealed or misrepresented some material facts relating to property being insured.

Further Readings on Insurance

(in addition to the sources cited in footnotes in this section)

Insurance Law in a Nutshell (Third Edition, 1996), by John F. Dobbyn

Hornbook on Insurance Law (1988), by Robert E. Keeton and Alan I. Widiss

Canadian Insurance Contracts Law in a Nutshell (1995), by Craig Brown

II.E. Protection of Intellectual Property Rights

II.E.1. Intellectual Property Rights

The term "intellectual property" refers to certain types of knowledge, expressions of ideas, or other creations that can be ascribed to a particular person or entity. According to one source, "[i]ntellectual property is, in essence, useful information or knowledge [and it comprises both] artistic property and industrial property." [64] In many countries, legal protection is provided for at least *three types of intellectual property*. Patent law protects inventions, trademark law protects brand names and designs, and copyright law protects writings (including films, recordings, and so forth). The first two of these (inventions and brand names or designs) constitute "industrial property", and the third one (writings) constitutes "artistic property". In addition, legal protection is sometimes provided for other types of intellectual property, including in particular industrial models and designs, trade secrets and "know-how", the layout ("topography") of integrated circuits, a famous individual's "personality", certain types of biological technology, and internet and electronic commerce technology.[65]

---

64. August-2000, *supra* note 1, at page 468.

65. See G. Gregory Letterman, BASICS OF INTERNATIONAL INTELLECTUAL PROPERTY LAW (2001), at page vii.

In all these cases, the fundamental purpose of the legal rules is to *protect the results of innovation and creation*, usually by providing a monopoly to the creator or owner of the right—that is, as one source has expressed it, by "enabling the owner [of the right] to prevent others from using and/or producing the protected invention, technology, or creative work".[66] Although several multilateral treaties have emerged in this area, most intellectual property law is essentially national law. That is, for the most part, intellectual property rights created within one nation's jurisdiction are completely absent (and therefore unenforceable) in every other nation's jurisdictions, unless a multilateral or bilateral treaty exists to provide otherwise. Even when treaties exist to protect intellectual property rights between nations, the scope and extent of such rights still usually vary from jurisdiction to jurisdiction.[67] For instance, economically developed countries might be more technologically capable and more economically inclined to provide more comprehensive intellectual property protection than economically less developed countries, which, due to their low technological and economic state of development, might feel that they benefit more from "free-riding" on the efforts of foreign creators.[68]

The following paragraphs identify the main themes of patent law, trademark law, and copyright law, indicating some of the elements of each and noting some of the main multilateral efforts that have been undertaken to coordinate the national laws.

II.E.2. Patents

Let us assume that after many years of research you have just invented a special piece of equipment that involves the passing of elec-

---

66. Melvin Simensky, Lanning G. Bryer, and Neil J. Wilkof, INTELLECTUAL PROPERTY IN THE GLOBAL MARKETPLACE (Vol. I) (John Wiley & Sons, 2nd edition, 1999), at page 0.5. The following paragraphs draw from that and other sources, including in particular Fred Abbott, Thomas Cottier, and Francis Gurry, THE INTERNATIONAL INTELLECTUAL PROPERTY SYSTEM (Part I) (Kluwer Law International, 1999), at pages 21–25, 81–84, and 128–131.

67. See Letterman, *supra* note 65, at pages 12–13.

68. *Id.* at pages 13–15.

trical current through a very thin wire inside a sealed glass enclosure. The wire glows, creating light. In other words, you have just invented a light bulb. It might occur to you to "protect" your invention, in either one of two different ways. First, you may wish to prevent other people from copying it and selling it, thereby enjoying financial rewards from work that you (not they) spent years doing. Alternatively, you may wish to prevent other people from knowing about your invention at all—perhaps because you want to use the light bulb only as a component in a larger product or process (for example, in creating special sound-and-light shows that will amaze audiences).

This fanciful example illustrates the difference between an invention and "industrial know-how", and therefore the different types of legal protection that might be afforded to each. The invention of the light bulb in this example could be "protected" as a legal matter under either patent or trade secret laws, but not both.[69] Under the rules most widely applicable around the world, a patent is a right granted to the inventor of a technological product or process that is new, useful, and "non-obvious". On the other hand, a trade secret is any information that provides a person with a competitive advantage so long as it remains a secret.[70]

In many countries, patent protection is provided by national legislation and various international conventions, discussed in further detail below; however, countries' legal protection of trade secrets varies widely, and very little international law exists on the topic. Because trade secrets do not have to be scrutinized to the extent that patents do in order to receive protection, trade secret protection is much easier to acquire;[71] however, if the information successfully meets the criteria for patent protection, i.e. it is new, useful, and "non-obvious", then patent law confers more comprehensive protection.[72] For this reason (and for many other commercial reasons, of course), creators usually choose to patent their inventions rather than to keep them secret.

---

69. See Roger D. Blair & Thomas F. Cotter, INTELLECTUAL PROPERTY: ECONOMIC AND LEGAL DIMENSIONS OF RIGHTS AND REMEDIES (2005), at page 7.

70. See *id.* at page 23.

71. See *id.* at pages 23–24.

72. See *id.* at page 7.

Each of the three required features of a patent—that is, that it be new, that it be useful, and that it be "non-obvious"—is important. The product or process must be new, or *novel*, in the sense that it has not already been invented, disclosed, or described by someone else. Questions often arise on this point. For example, how much difference must there be between a particular type of light bulb that has already been invented and patented and a new type of light bulb, in order to warrant protection? National laws on patent protection provide definitions to answer such questions.

Likewise, national laws establish standards on how *useful* an invention has to be in order to be granted patent rights. Although it might be assumed that some commercial use could be found for almost any invention, some recent developments in the fields of chemistry and biotechnology have yielded new molecules and compounds that do not seem to have any immediate use. Typically, mere speculation about some possible utility in the future will not be sufficient to obtain patent protection. Similarly, a common rule is that an invention cannot be patented if it is merely a curiosity with no real benefit. Under this rule, it is usually not possible to obtain patent rights for illegal, immoral, or dangerous items.

The last of the three required features—that an invention must be "*non-obvious*" in order to obtain patent protection—means that the new product or process is not simply an elementary or apparent improvement over an existing product or process. Assume, for example, that someone is granted a patent for a light bulb that works well in most respects but does not work in certain types of sockets because the heat it creates sometimes damages the socket or switch mechanism. Separate patent protection typically would not be granted for another light bulb that includes more heat insulation around the base so as to guard against such damage to the socket or switch mechanism. A new light bulb of that sort might be new and useful, but it is probably too obvious to qualify for a separate patent. In short, an invention typically is not patentable unless it represents some advance over the "prior art" so that an ordinary mechanic skilled in that prior art would not have been capable of making the advance as an obvious or straightforward modification.

Once a patent has been granted, the patentee typically will enjoy (for a prescribed period of time) an *exclusive right* to make, use, or sell the invention. In some countries, this includes the right to refrain from using the invention. In many countries, however, the inventor is obligated to "work" the patent; if the inventor does not do that, he can be required to grant a compulsory license to others who wish to exploit the invention.

Why would such rights—that is, the exclusive rights over one's own invention—be provided? There are two predominant *theoretical foundations* for the granting of patent rights. One of them draws from European history and the centralization of commerce:

> Beginning in medieval times, certain segments of European commerce became centralized and exclusively controlled by various groups. The most notable of these were the early guilds, each of which controlled, at least partially, particular areas of commerce, such as leatherworking, glassmaking and manufactured goods.... In time, the right to control various sectors of the market became a royal privilege, granted by the monarch in return for various benefits. These early 'patent' monopolies were not concerned with invention, but, rather, with commerce.[73]

Another theoretical foundation for the granting of patent rights focuses on incentives. Granting patent rights prevents what is called "free-riding" and preserves an economic incentive to create. Inventions are public goods; almost everyone can benefit from them (take a "free ride" on them), directly or indirectly, regardless of whether they pay a fair market price for the benefits. This "free-riding" problem risks undermining the incentives that a person would otherwise have to commit the time or money necessary to create, disclose, and commercialize new inventions, unless patent protection laws regulate the control of access to the invention and ensure that inventors are financially compensated for their efforts.[74]

---

73. Arthur R. Miller and Michael H. Davis, INTELLECTUAL PROPERTY IN A NUTSHELL (West, 3d edition, 2000) at pages 5–6. This source has also been used in preparing the foregoing paragraphs.

74. See Blair & Cotter, *supra* note 69, at page 15.

On the strength of that reasoning, it has long been recognized that without the incentive of exclusive use, an inventor might never share his or her invention with the public. In other words, in order for society at large to benefit from the creativeness of certain individuals, those individuals must be rewarded for their inventiveness. However, since many legal systems also reflect the belief that monopolies can bring economic harm to society, patent rights typically are limited to a specified number of years. After that period of time has run, the patent enters the "public domain", which means that anyone else then has the right to make, use, or sell the invention.

A key *multilateral agreement* relating to patents is the Paris Convention for the Protection of Industrial Property. That treaty, which entered into force in its original form over a century ago (July 1884), emerged after a great many bilateral treaties had been adopted among countries to provide for reciprocal protection of patent rights. The Paris Convention, as revised most recently in 1967, provides that an inventor from one member country who applies for a patent in another member country will receive national treatment—that is, the same treatment that a citizen of that country receives. Moreover, the treaty also grants certain procedural advantages, including special filing priority (twelve months) to an inventor from one member country intending to apply for a patent in another member country. This is an important procedural right because in many countries the simple act of filing an application publicizes the invention, making it ineligible for patent protection in other countries that require absolute novelty of an invention (including lack of publication) in order to receive a patent.

Other multilateral treaties also apply to patents. For example, the Patent Cooperation Treaty, which dates from 1970, establishes procedural rules by which applicants for patents can preserve their priority and gain a head start on filing in other countries. In Europe, the European Patent Convention allows applicants for patents to choose to be examined by a central authority that makes a decision on patentability and issues a European patent—although it is still necessary to register formally for a separate patent in each EU member country.

Some of the multilateral treaties referred to in the preceding paragraphs have gained greater importance in the last few years because of the Uruguay Round of trade negotiations, discussed below starting in subsection C.2. of Chapter IV. One of the agreements emerging from the Uruguay Round, which concluded in 1993, was the so-called *TRIPs Agreement*—the Agreement on Trade-Related Aspects of Intellectual Property Rights. It incorporates some of the rules of the Paris Convention, as well as some other treaties (referred to below) regarding trademarks and copyright. In order to become a member of the World Trade Organization, a country must accept the TRIPs Agreement; accordingly, most countries in the world have accepted that treaty. (Whether a particular country actually adheres to the rules set forth in that treaty is a separate matter.)

II.E.3. Trademarks

A trademark is a *sign, mark, or design*[75] that is used on or in connection with the marketing of a product or service in order to distinguish the owner's product or service from those of other persons. Under typical intellectual property rules, no person other than the trademark owner may use the protected trademark (or any similar mark) in a way that would tend to confuse the public. Expressed differently, this means that "[t]rademark laws confer on the proprietor [of the trademark] the exclusive right to prevent all third parties not having the consent of the owner from using in the course of trade any sign which is identical with the trademark" or so similar to it as to make a consumer think it is the same.[76]

It has been suggested that a trademark has traditionally performed *four main functions*. First, it distinguishes the products of one enterprise from products of other enterprises, thus helping a consumer to identify a product that was already known to him or her. Second, it refers to a particular quality of products for which the trademark is used. Third, it relates a particular product to the producer, thus indicating the origin of the product. Fourth, it promotes the market-

---

75. The operative words of the definition offered in US law are "word, name, symbol, or device".

76. Abbott et al, *supra* note 66, at page 129.

ing and sale of products. The second and third of these traditional functions are less important today.

As can be seen from these four traditional functions, trademark law provides *two types of protection.* For one thing, it can protect the trademark owner from "trademark dilution", or losing the benefit of goodwill that he or she has been able to build up in the minds of consumers who recognize his or her product through quality control and advertising. Second, trademark law can also protect the public from "consumer confusion", or the confusion that could result when one person uses the same mark or design that another well-known person has already developed and used to distinguish his or her own products. Of course, a counterclaim to "consumer confusion" is "reverse confusion": when a trademark infringer is not marketing competitive products or services and consumers are not likely to be confused into thinking that the infringer produces similar products or services as the rightful trademark owner, then the infringer might suffer harm if enjoined from infringing on the trademark; in such a case the infringer might be given a limited right to continue infringing on the trademark.[77] For example, if James McDonald operates a stained glass repair shop in Ireland and calls it McDonald's, he may suffer harm if the restaurant franchise McDonald's tries to enjoin him from using its name.

The sign, mark, or design constituting the trademark may consist of one or more distinctive words, letters, numbers, pictures, drawings, or distinctive form (for example, the shape of a Coca-Cola bottle). In certain cases, and in certain countries, even a specific color can constitute a trademark, or at least its use can be protected as constituting a key feature of a trademark. However, trademark laws typically offer no protection for the use of "generic" words, signs, or marks—that is, those that are already in the public domain because they are commonly used in society (such as the word "car").

In order to register a trademark, and thus gain legal protection for its use, a person typically needs to show that he or she has already used the trademark in commerce; this requirement is consistent with

---

77. See Blair & Cotter, *supra* note 69, at page 34.

the theory that a trademark is already recognizable by the consuming public. However, in some countries (including the USA) it is also possible to register a trademark simply by demonstrating an intention to use it in the future in marketing a product. In that case, the applicant would still need to show that nobody else is entitled to use the trademark and that the applicant's use of the trademark would not cause confusion.

The closest thing to an international trademark is the protection offered by the Madrid Agreement Concerning the International Registration of Marks and the subsequent Madrid Protocol.[78] The Madrid Agreement, first prepared in 1891 and updated over the years, grants *automatic registration* of a trademark in all member countries once the trademark is registered in the country of origin. Under the Madrid Agreement, the owner of a home country trademark registration may file an international application with its national trademark office designating those other member countries in which extension of protection is desired. The international application is then forwarded to the World Intellectual Property Organization, which issues an international registration for the mark and forwards the application to the designated countries. Under the Madrid Protocol, adopted in 1989, this international registration procedure could be started as soon as a home country application (as opposed to a home country registration) is made. The Paris Convention, discussed above in connection with patent rights, also provides certain procedural advantages (a filing priority of six months) in respect of trademark protection.

As with patent rights, trademark rights also are affected by the widespread adoption of the TRIPs Agreement emerging from the Uruguay Round of trade negotiations (see subsection E.2., above). Some provisions of the treaties referred to above, in particular those in the Paris Convention relating to trademarks, are incorporated by reference into the TRIPs Agreement.

---

78. The details given in this paragraph, and some in the preceding paragraphs, are drawn primarily from Miller and Davis, *supra* note 73, at pages 435–436.

II.E.4. Copyright[79]

The protection of "copyright" applies, in a very general sense, to writings. In most countries, copyright protection extends beyond mere writings, however, to include all original works—literary, dramatic, musical, or artistic—that are fixed in any tangible means of expression. Copyright protection is often extended, for example, to sculpture, videotape, recorded choreography, and computer programs.

Two fundamental building blocks of copyright law are the concepts of *expression* and *originality*. The concept of expression means that only ideas *as they are expressed* are copyrightable. Another way of describing this principle is that ideas in and of themselves are not protectable under copyright law. (This principle is similar to the principle in patent law, discussed above, that legal protection is only extended to the novel, useful, and non-obvious *application* of an idea.) The concept of originality means that the work must have originated with the author; the author cannot have copied it from another.

Once granted, copyright protects authors and artists against the unauthorized copying or reproduction of their creative expression. The protection afforded by copyright is typically longer than that given by patents—often for the life of the author or artist plus some number of years. However, throughout the life of the copyright, exceptions typically are made from the prohibition on copying. For example, the right of "fair use" often permits portions of otherwise copyrighted works to be used for instruction purposes.

Computer technology has made it possible to transform expressive works into electronic form, which has in turn made it possible to reproduce those works easily and inexpensively. This development gives more urgency to an old question: how should the benefits available to society from the easy distribution of information and culture be balanced against the interests of copyright holders who fear loss of control over their expressive works?

---

79. Material in this subsection draws primarily from Abbott et al, *supra* note 66, at pages 81–84, Miller and Davis, *supra* note 73, at pages 292–294 and 433, and Simensky et al, *supra* note 66, at pages 0.7–0.8.

The answer to this question may turn in part on the *theory* underlying copyright protection. Why should a legal system provide such protection? According to one source, "[c]opyright exists to reward creators for creating works and disclosing them to the public and to foster a cultural sensitivity and identity."[80] A somewhat different theoretical approach (emphasized somewhat more in European law) rests on the notion of "moral rights" that authors and artists are viewed as having in their works. Such moral rights, which are thought to be inalienable (that is, not capable of being sold), include the right to prevent a mutilation or other abuse of the work that would disparage the reputation of the author.

At the *international level*, the Berne Convention for the Protection of Literary and Artistic Works (1886) is one of the treaties that govern copyright. The Berne Convention, which refers to "moral rights" as discussed in the preceding paragraph, guarantees national treatment and sets some minimum standards for copyright protection among its member countries. More specifically, the Berne Convention establishes *three key principles*:

- the *national treatment* principle—works originating in one Berne Convention member country must be given the same protection in each of the other member countries as they grant to the works of their own nationals;
- the principle of *automatic protection*—the protection mentioned above must not be conditional upon compliance with any formalities; and
- the principle of *independence of protection*—the protection mentioned above is independent of the existence of protection in the country of origin of the work.

As in the case of patent and trademark, copyright protection at the *international level* is affected importantly by the TRIPs Agreement emerging from the Uruguay Round of trade negotiations. Thus, even those countries (including, for example, the USA) that had not ac-

---

80. Simensky et al, *supra* note 66, at page 0.7.

ceded to the Berne Convention earlier are now subject to some of its key provisions.[81]

The above descriptions of multilateral developments relating to intellectual property protection included references to the World Intellectual Property Organization ("*WIPO*"). WIPO was established by a 1967 treaty and became a Specialized Agency of the United Nations in 1974. Its activities center on facilitating the registration of intellectual property rights, the progressive development of intellectual property law, and the resolving of disputes among states that are parties to intellectual property treaties. Those treaties include the ones referred to in the preceding paragraphs—for example, the Paris Convention, the Madrid Agreement, and the Berne Convention—as well as over a dozen other treaties.[82]

Further Readings on Intellectual Property Law

(in addition to the sources cited in footnotes in this section)

Intellectual Property World Desk Reference (looseleaf), by Thomas M.S. Hemnes

Intellectual Property in a Nutshell (Third Edition, 2000), by Arthur R. Miller and Michael H. Davis

Basics of International Intellectual Property Law (2001), by G. Gregory Letterman

The International Intellectual Property System (1999), by Frederick Abbott, Thomas Cottier, and Francis Gurry

Intellectual Property in the Global Marketplace (1999), by Melvin Simensky, Lanning Bryer, and Neil J. Wilkof

International Copyright (2001), by Paul Goldstein

International Copyright Law and Practice (looseleaf), by Melville B. Nimmer and Paul Edward Geller

---

81. For a brief description of the TRIPs Agreement, see Jentz et al, *supra* note 43, at pages 153–156.

82. For further details on WIPO and intellectual property treaties, see Abbot et al, *supra* note 66, at pages 303–308.

The International Protection of Designs (2000), by Denis Cohen

Copyright—National and International Development, by Stig Strigholm, in International Encyclopaedia of Comparative Law, vol. XIV, chap. 2 (1990)

Copyright and Industrial Property—General Questions—The International Conventions, by Eugen Ulmer, in International Encyclopaedia of Comparative Law, vol. XIV, chap. 1 (1987). See also August-2000, *supra* note 1, at Chapter 9

II.F. Cyber Law

Cyber law may be seen as a "cross-cutting" topic, because it cuts across numerous areas of law—commercial law, intellectual property, financial law, criminal law, international law, and others—but from a specific perspective that arises out of very recent technological developments. Those technological developments are variously described as the "information revolution", the rise of the world wide web, and the development of "cyberspace".

Until recently, there has been a conflict between *two competing viewpoints* regarding the legal implications of these technological developments. On the one hand, some commentators (and government officials) have taken the view that the dramatic developments in information technology are so great as to require brand-new types of regulation. On the other hand, others have taken the position that while the technological changes are indeed dramatic, the legal implications of those changes can fairly easily be accommodated by existing legal concepts, institutions, and rules.

Although the conflict between these two viewpoints has not been completely resolved, it does appear that momentum is moving toward the first one—that the technological revolution that has occurred does require some departure from existing legal rules and doctrines and the development of entirely new ones. However, there is considerable uncertainty and disagreement about precisely what changes are needed and what the content of the new rules and doctrines should be.

Accordingly, the following paragraphs identify some of the key issues that make up "cyber law" today. Little attempt is made here to posit the specific rules, because the legal landscape in this area is currently so uncertain and changing so quickly. Instead, the primary aim of these descriptions is to highlight questions that national and multinational legal systems will need to address.

II.F.1. Governance of Cyberspace

One key issue in cyber law regards government regulation — whether there should be any such regulation, and if so what government institutions should be entrusted to provide it. Unlike most other forms of activity, "cyber-activity" does not take place (to the same degree) within the territorial sovereignty of any particular state.

Let us examine this by posing a hypothetical example. If Cherry Chum sends an e-mail message to a friend in another country, or searches the internet for information about the explorer Ferdinand Magellan, or orders a book from Amazon.com, or visits the website of *Playboy* magazine, his activity not only crosses national borders but remains in some sense outside those borders. That being the case, what government entity, if any, has legal authority to regulate the content of the e-mail message, or to monitor the fees charged for using an internet search engine (or the advertisements that accompany it), or to settle commercial disputes arising out of the agreement by Amazon.com to sell the book, or to protect against pornography appearing on someone's website?

There are two views on who should govern "cyber-activity" and how jurisdiction should be drawn in cyberspace. One view argues that cyberspace cannot legitimately be governed by territorially based sovereigns and that the online world should be its own legal jurisdiction, or even multiple jurisdictions. On the other hand, the opposite view, supported largely by national governments, argues that territorially based laws should govern any conceivable online activity.[83]

---

83. See Patricia L. Bellia et al., CYBERLAW: PROBLEMS OF POLICY AND JURISPRUDENCE IN THE INFORMATION AGE (2003), at page 63.

An important analysis of cyberspace jurisdiction appeared a decade ago in the US court case of *Zippo Mfg. Co. v. Zippo Dot Com, Inc.*[84] The *Zippo* court defined jurisdiction over websites along a spectrum, with three main categories.

At one end of the spectrum are *passive websites*, which supply information accessible to anyone surfing the Internet. Examples include informational or advertising websites, such as university websites. Passive websites typically would not trigger jurisdiction in a foreign nation because they do not avail themselves of the foreign market. However, foreign governments can prohibit their own citizens from visiting certain websites containing content banned under their own laws.[85]

In the middle of the spectrum are *interactive websites*, which post information accessible to anyone surfing the Internet, but also conduct a limited amount of interactive activities. Considerable uncertainty surrounds whether interactive websites should trigger foreign jurisdiction. Courts judge this issue on a case-by-case basis, depending upon the type and frequency of the website's cyberspace activities, as well as other factors.

At the other end of the spectrum are *highly interactive or commercial websites*, which purposefully direct activity into a foreign jurisdiction. Highly interactive or commercial websites are generally seen as triggering jurisdiction in a foreign nation and are subject to foreign regulation, liability, and judicial determination of their rights. For example, if a shoe company in the Philippines sells its shoes exclusively to Canada via its website, sends out advertising emails to Canadian email addresses, establishes affiliate programs with Canadian business websites, etc., then the shoe company will be subject to jurisdiction in Canada.

To answer our hypothetical example above, national governments typically will try to impose regulation over some or all of these activities in which Cherry Chum is engaged—sending e-mail messages, buying a book, conducting research, seeing the Playboy website—

---

84. 952 F.Supp. 1119 (W.D. Pa. 1997).
85. See John W. Bagby, CYBERLAW HANDBOOK FOR E-COMMERCE (2003), at page 21. The following two paragraphs also draw liberally from this source.

but it remains uncertain whether such regulations in fact are enforced. As a practical matter, governments typically will be unable to impose effective regulation over some or all of these activities in which Cherry Chum is engaged. Indeed, to the extent that one national government would try to do so, one or more other national governments are likely to object on grounds that such regulations would impinge on their own sovereignty. Likewise, attempts by multilateral government institutions (such as the United Nations, for example) to impose regulations on such activities also will probably be met with resistance by national governments.

Even non-governmental organizations, such as the Internet Corporation for Assigned Names and Numbers (ICANN) or even "eBay" (an online auction company), can and do regulate cyberspace. However, there are disadvantages and advantages to cyberspace regulation by non-governmental organizations. One disadvantage is that because the regulation is non-governmental, there is no guarantee of appropriate oversight or due process in the regulatory activities. On the other hand, one advantage is that the regulation is more flexible because it does not rely on top-down governmental solutions.[86]

In addition, resistance to regulation of such "cyber-activity" will come from citizens or users themselves, on a variety of grounds. For example, regulation of e-mail correspondence would in many societies run afoul of legal guarantees and expectations of the freedom of expression or the right to privacy.

Indeed, the very nature of "cyber-activity" raises both practical and conceptual issues relating to the overall question of governance—that is, relating to how behavior on the internet will be regulated. One source makes the following observations in this regard:

> [T]he Internet is arguably regulated as much by non-state entities (such as independent service providers or bodies that set technical standards) as it is by formal sovereign governments. Moreover, individual identities can be transformed through the anonymity, malleability and easy access to public space that are pervasive features of the technology. Pri-

---

86. See Bellia et al., *supra* note 83, at page 333.

vate consensual arrangements among individuals and groups, whether by contract or custom, also substitute for formal governance mechanisms.… Finally, law itself is problematized by Internet technology. Traditionally, law involves a centralized sovereign actor that exerts power within its territorial boundaries. However, several features of the Internet combine to disrupt this framework: the instantaneous extraterritoriality of most acts, the lack of centralized power, and the fluidity of geographic or political boundaries. To a much greater degree than with other technologies, the design choices made by engineers will also act as a type of "regulation". [Hence, there are some important] challenges posed to the concept of law by Internet technology.[87]

II.F.2. Rights and Freedoms in Cyberspace

Although the new technology of cyberspace raises many issues specifically relating to individual rights and freedoms, three in particular stand out as most important: (i) the right to intellectual property protection, (ii) the freedom of expression, and (iii) the right to privacy. The following paragraphs touch on these issues briefly.

As for the right to *intellectual property protection*, several questions arise:

- Who, if anyone "owns" the content that travels through cyberspace, and what rights arise from such ownership?
- How much control should content owners have over the use and dissemination of their works over the internet? Proponents of strong copyright protection argue that, because of the remarkable ease with which digital material can be "copied" and transmitted over the internet, the law should provide more and better tools to prevent members of the public from "copying"

---

87. Maggie Chon, *Introduction to Cyberspace*, appearing as a module on Learning Cyberlaw in Cyberspace, available at www.cyberspacelaw.org.

writings, music, and other works without the author's permission. However, opponents of this view challenge the notion that digital transmissions constitute "copies" at all, and argue that the public should be allowed to share, lend, and pass on digital materials just as they have traditionally done with copies of books, music, etc.

• What liability, if any, should internet service providers have for infringement of copyright initiated by their subscribers?

Some answers to these questions have been attempted in some countries. In the USA, for example, the Digital Millennium Copyright Act was enacted in late 1998, creating a "sea-change" in US copyright law as it relates to new digital technology—and creating a chorus of criticism as well, on grounds that it gave the wrong answer to the wrong questions.[88] Legal developments are also taking place in respect of the protection of other intellectual property rights in the context of the internet and the electronic revolution.[89]

In the area of *freedom of expression*, many countries are struggling with the question of where to strike a balance between government regulation (to the extent that such regulation is even possible in the case of "cyber-activity") and the human right of free speech. That right is enshrined in many national constitutions and statutes, and is a key feature of several human rights treaties that have nearly universal participation. However, the internet holds almost unlimited potential for conveying inflammatory speech, threatening speech, defamation, hate speech, and even calls for overthrow of a government—all without easy attribution to any particular person whose conduct can be kept within socially or politically acceptable limits. As a result, several countries—China is an example—find difficulty in imposing the level of control that they want over "cyber-activity".

---

88. See, e.g., Jay Dratler, Jr., CYBERLAW: INTELLECTUAL PROPERTY IN THE DIGITAL MILLENNIUM (Law Journal Press, 2002), at pages v–x.

89. For a discussion of such developments, see Jentz et al, *supra* note 43, at pages 150–156. Those authors address issues regarding intellectual property rights in domain names and in certain cyber-products such as data-compression software, encryption programs, and the like.

The question of regulation also arises in the area of *privacy*. One author has made this observation about privacy in cyberspace:

> One of the real "sleeper" political issues generated by the popularity of the Internet is privacy, or the ability of consumers to control what information about them others may be able to view or gain access to on the Net. Privacy advocates claim that on the Net, there is not much privacy at all. The mere act of visiting a website generally triggers the placement of "cookies" on an individual's computer. These cookies enable the website to welcome back a visitor, but they also allow the operators of that website to read from the cookie what other websites an individual has visited. This information may be sold to third parties or kept by the website itself to ascertain consumer preferences and target new product offerings.[90]

The European approach has been to take preventive measures: the EU Directive on Data Protection (Directive 95/46/EC, effective October 1998) controls the gathering and use of personal data, as well as any subsequent dissemination of that information. Under the Directive, a company that gathers personal information—for example, from an individual who visits a website online—must first obtain the individual's permission and explain how the information will be used; and the company cannot then use the information for any other purpose. Furthermore, the Directive gives individuals a right to see information on file with the company and to correct or delete the information; it also gives an individual a right to bring legal action against anyone who misuses the information (as defined in the Directive).[91]

While the European approach, described above, rests on a philosophy that the government should intervene to protect the privacy of citizens, the American approach has generally been more reactive in

---

90. Robert E. Litan, *Law and Policy in the Age of the Internet*, 50 Duke Law Journal 1045 (2001), at pages 1057–1058.

91. For several accounts of the EU Directive on Data Protection, see Folsom et al, *supra* note 43, at pages 187–196. The description given here draws heavily from that source.

character—that is, providing legal remedies if an individual can prove, after the fact, that he or she has suffered some injury as a result of privacy invasion. The conflict between the two approaches has created considerable friction, particularly because the EU Directive threatened to impose the equivalent of a "data embargo" on the export of personal information about EU citizens to countries that did not, in the judgment of the EU, provide adequate protections of such information.

II.F.3. Cybercrime

Perhaps any new environment invites criminal activity. In earlier centuries, the exploration and settling of new territories gave rise to outlaws. Similarly, with the opening of the new "territory" of cyberspace, it appears that a great many individuals have yielded to the temptations of criminal activity. Such criminal activity, in the context of cyberspace, can take many forms. National governments and international agencies are just beginning to fight such crimes effectively and to provide protection from the crimes and the criminals who commit them.

The *range of cybercrimes* includes the following types of activity:[92]

- *fraud*—especially fraud in financial transactions conducted over the internet or electronically. In one recent case, a woman falsely promised to sell users of the on-line auction company "eBay" various items, including jewelry, musical instruments, car parts and electronic goods. When the eBay users arranged to buy these items, the woman instructed them to pay for the merchandise via wire transfers to her bank account. She never sent the goods.
- *illegal gambling*—this gambling has also recently become a serious cybercrime, for several reasons. First, local law enforcement officials have great difficulty detecting and tracing the act of and those involved with illegal online gambling, which often operates on money laundering by organized criminals. Second, illegal online gambling often involves foreign nations where the

---

92. Most of the types of cybercrime listed here are drawn from information appearing on the cybercrime portion of the website of the US Department of Justice, at www.usdoj.gov/criminal/cybercrime.

gambling is legal, which introduces the jurisdictional issues discussed above.[93]

- *illegal copyright infringement*—for example, by producing and selling illegally reproduced software.

- *malicious computer "spamming"*—for example, sending thousands of email messages in order to overload a company's computer server.

- *identity theft*—that is, gaining enough personal information about a person, through electronic means, to pretend to be that person and enter into transactions as that person.

- *drug-related crimes*—for example, distribution of controlled drugs through internet "prescriptions".

- *unauthorized access to computer files*—or "hacking", usually for the purpose of gaining information or conducting illegal financial transactions. This is also sometimes called cyberterrorism. For example, an American recently admitted to illegally accessing the computer system of his former employer and reading the e-mail messages of company executives for the purpose of gaining a commercial advantage at his new job at a competitor company.

- *spreading computer "viruses"*—as was done by a New Jersey man who unleashed the "Melissa" computer virus in 1999, causing millions of dollars in damage and infecting untold numbers of computers and computer networks.

- *other internet crimes of a financial nature*—for example, tax evasion.

- *computer crimes creating death or serious physical injury*—for example, by interference with computer systems that are essential components in providing basic services such as electric power, emergency response, telecommunications, or medical care; disruption of those systems can have a catastrophic effect.

- *cyber-stalking*—a practice in which the stalker intercepts the victim's email and Internet activity to harass or threaten the victim's family or damage the victim's property. Often, the stalker poses as a friendly, non-threatening correspondent in chat

---

93. Bagby, *supra* note 85, at page 87.

rooms or other communications. Children are especially vulnerable to cyberstalking by pedophiles and other predatory adults, who gain the children's trust and then persuade them to send revealing pictures or messages, or even to lure the children to unprotected places where they may suffer physical, emotional, or other harm.[94]

Many countries are having difficulty fighting these various forms of cybercrime. Even more challenging, perhaps, than fighting cybercrime at the national level, however, is fighting cybercrime at the *international level*. Some of this challenge arises because of inadequate coordination of laws and law-enforcement efforts. For example, if one country's laws criminalize certain activities on computers and another country's laws do not, cooperation in solving a crime and prosecuting the perpetrator may not be possible. A criminal might weave his communications through three, four, or five countries before reaching his intended victims. In that case, inadequate laws in just one of those countries can, in effect, shield that criminal from law enforcement around the world. Moreover, multilateral arrangements for investigating and prosecuting cybercrime are needed.

In response to these needs, several multilateral steps have recently been taken. For example, a Convention on Cyber Crime was prepared in 2000. It takes steps toward (i) harmonizing the substantive national laws in the area of computer crime, (ii) empowering domestic law enforcement officials with procedural authority to obtain electronic evidence within their territorial jurisdiction, and (iii) developing mechanisms for expedited international legal assistance in the investigation and prosecution of computer crimes. Earlier, in 1997 and 1998, considerable work was done in the context of the so-called "G-8" ministerial and heads-of-state meetings to agree on a joint plan to fight cyber crime, as laid out in a set of ten Principles and a ten-point Action Plan adopted in December 1997.[95]

---

94. See *id.* at pages 85–86.
95. See various speeches and reports appearing on the cybercrime portion of the website of the US Department of Justice, www.usdoj.gov/criminal/cybercrime.

Further Readings on Cyber Law

(in addition to the sources cited in footnotes in this section)

Cyberlaw: Intellectual Property in the Digital Millennium (looseleaf, 2000), by Jay Dratler

Learning Cyberlaw in Cyberspace (1999), available at www.cyber-spacelaw.org

Liberating Cyberspace—Civil Liberties, Human Rights and the Internet (1999), edited by the National Council for Civil Liberties (UK)

Governing the Internet (2001), by Marcus Franda

Governance in 'Cyberspace' (1999), by Klaus W. Grewlich

Chapter III

The Role of Government in the Economy

The materials in Chapters I and II focus primarily on the private sector. In a modern market-based economic system, it is largely the private business entities that provide the fuel for economic activity and growth. Indeed, this is both an ideological and a practical lesson that most countries have now embraced—that private sector activity, carried out in the context of a market-based economy, is far superior to a centrally-planned economy. Hence it makes sense to refer first (in section A of Chapter I) to the various forms of business organization, and thereafter to concentrate on the methods by which business entities obtain financing, record their financial affairs, enter into contracts, settle their disputes, insure against risk, and so on.

But government also has a very important role to play in an economic system. In order for a market-based system to work efficiently, a wide range of rules must be established and enforced to assure that the operations of business entities are carried out fairly and honestly. Typically the job of establishing and enforcing those rules rests with the government. The role of government varies, obviously, from one country to another, not only in the scope of its involvement in regulating the economy but also in the details of the rules it establishes and enforces.

The aim of this Chapter, therefore, is mainly to describe five key areas of government regulation and to identify some of the important *issues* that the rules address, without attempting to explain the detailed substantive *rules* themselves. The first area discussed is labor law—rules governing the relationship between employers and employees, designed in part to protect the well-being of workers who typically have less concentrated bargaining power than do the employers they work for. The second area is natural resources and environmental law—rules to protect the common resources of the country against the temptation of individuals and business entities to waste or pollute them for short-term gain. The third area regards rules to protect consumers against various dangers from business entities, especially manufacturers (consumer protection and product liability). The fourth topic raised is tax law, which serves both to generate the revenue needed to fund the government's efforts at regulation and in some cases to direct resources into areas that the government regards as important to the economic and social life of the country. The last topic covered in this Chapter—the role of the government in protecting the economy against corruption and terrorism—reflects some recent technological and political developments that are international in scope and importance.

III.A. Labor Law

III.A.1. General Observations

Labor law has its *foundation in contract law.* The relationship that exists between an employer and an employee is a contractual relationship. However, it is also more than that. From the perspective of the employee, the employment contract is typically the principal means of producing income. From the perspective of the employer, the employment contract represents one of the largest components of cost in conducting business. For these and other reasons, the employment relationship is typically among the most heavily regulated areas of business operations.

Many variations in labor law exist among nations. For example, Europe's labor structure can be characterized generally as a welfare state system; Japan's as a paternalistic system; and that of the USA as a decentralized bargaining system. While labor unions and company managers in the USA usually negotiate fringe benefits, such as vacations, employment compensation, and medical insurance, on an individual or group basis, European governments deal with such matters legislatively. Furthermore, in contrast to both the USA and

Europe—where the termination of employment can occur "at will", or can be negotiated collectively, or can be regulated by legislation or caselaw—Japanese companies often offer lifetime employment for "permanent" employees, without inducement by labor unions or legislation.[96] In Australia, labor laws are similar to Western Europe and the EU, while its neighbor, New Zealand, recently revised its labor laws, weakening unions and revising wages, all in hopes that it would become more competitive in the global marketplace. In the Middle East, particularly in countries with Islamic legal systems, such as Saudi Arabia and Iran, labor law incorporates religious issues. In Africa, labor law is extremely varied, with some countries having no labor law at all.[97]

III.A.2. Issues Covered in Labor Legislation

Although the details of labor law vary, sometimes dramatically, from one country to the next, labor laws in most countries do typically address certain key aspects of the employment relationship. These include types or forms of labor relationships, terms of employment contracts, working conditions, unemployment compensation, working conditions, and labor-management relations.

First, labor laws usually distinguish between *different types of labor relationships.* A major distinction in this regard is between (i) an employee hired to perform work on a continuing (usually full-time) basis (either for an indefinite duration or for a relatively long fixed term), under the ongoing control or supervision of the employer and having a close connection with the business entity itself[98] and (ii) a person hired as a more independent occasional worker, somewhat

---

96. See William B. Gould IV, A Primer on American Labor Law (4th ed. 2004), at pages 3,6.

97. See Nancy J. Sedmak, *Employment Law Around the Globe, in* International Employment Law: The Multinational Employer and the Global Workforce (Dennis Campbell et al., eds., 1999), at page 11.

98. For a definition of "worker" in the laws of the European Union, see Roger Blanpain and Chris Engels, European Labour Law (Kluwer, 1993), at page 98. They write that "[t]he essential feature of an employment relation ... is the fact

"outside" the business entity, for a specific project. An example of the first would be a secretary hired to work in a business office, or a salesman assisting customers in making purchases from the business. An example of the second—referred to as an "independent contractor" in some systems—would be a self-employed electrician hired to install new wiring for a computer system in an office building, or an outside management consultant engaged to carry out a short-term assessment of the organizational structure of the business entity. Typically, labor laws do not apply (or they apply only partially) to the second of these two types of labor relationships. Because such an "independent contractor" does not rely on a single employer for a livelihood, government regulation of the employment relationship is less important.

Second, labor laws typically prescribe some of the *terms of an employment contract.* One author has described the situation in this way:

> In the usual contracting situation, the parties negotiate their own arrangement. They decide (1) whether they wish to enter into the relationship, and, if so, (2) on what terms. While the parties to an employment contract are generally still in control of the first decision, they have lost some control over the second. [Labor] laws now impose regulations on the terms of the employment contract.[99]

The terms thus regulated by legislation in many countries will relate to such things as these:

- the hours a person may work in one day or in one week;
- the minimum wages that a person must be paid, and any automatic cost-of-living adjustments that must be provided;
- the minimum age of a person who can be hired as a worker;
- the provision of training to employees;
- the grounds on which an employee may be dismissed;
- maternal, paternal, and parental leave rights;

---

that for a certain period of time a person performs services for and under the direction of another person in return for which he receives remuneration."

99. Cameron, *supra* note 1, at page 414 (numbering added).

- various social benefits that an employer must provide to an employee, such as assistance in paying for medical insurance and life insurance; and
- methods to be followed in resolving labor disputes.

Third, labor laws typically require employers to provide reasonably *safe working conditions* for their employees. Labor laws sometimes also make employers responsible for injuries suffered by employees if the safety standards have not been observed.[100]

Other issues addressed by labor laws—but addressed differently in different countries, of course—include (i) unemployment compensation (payments made available from a fund administered by the government for the benefit of workers who have temporarily lost their jobs because of economic and industry downturns), (ii) labor-management relations and bargaining power (guaranteeing the right of labor unions to organize and bargain with management, and sometimes establishing a separate set of dispute resolution rules and tribunals)[101], (iii) management and industry relations with local governments (ensuring that employment operations comply with foreign employment laws and drafting corporate "codes of conduct"),[102] and (iv) employment discrimination (prohibiting employers from discriminating unfairly against a worker on account of race, gender, religion, or other similar grounds in decisions to hire, fire, or promote).

III.A.3. International Labor Law

Many of these standards and requirements derive from *international agreements*. More than 150 agreements have been sponsored

---

100. See Donald C. Dowling, Jr., *International Labor and Employment Law—Practice and Consulting, in* INTERNATIONAL EMPLOYMENT LAW: THE MULTINATIONAL EMPLOYER AND THE GLOBAL WORKFORCE (Dennis Campbell et al., eds., 1999), at page 11.

101. For a survey of laws and procedures in various countries regarding these issues, see Benjamin Aaron, *Labor Courts and Organs of Arbitration, in* INTERNATIONAL ENCYCLOPEDIA OF COMPARATIVE LAW (Vol. XV, Ch. 16) (Oceana Publications, 1985).

102. See Dowling, *supra* note 100, at page 11.

by the International Labour Organization ("ILO") since it was founded in 1919 following World War I. The primary goals of the ILO are the improvement of working conditions, the raising of living standards, and the fair and equitable treatment of workers in all countries. To achieve these goals, the ILO has adopted a great many standards and recommendations that have international effect. Why should they have such international effect? One writer cites three main reasons:

> The first, and most practical, is that individual states are not inclined to enact domestic labor laws because this would put them at a competitive disadvantage in the world market by increasing local labor costs. The adoption of an internationally effective agreement would, accordingly, keep multinational companies from practicing what is sometimes called "social dumping." Second, the establishment of fair and equitable labor standards helps promote world peace. Third, the establishment of uniform labor standards is a matter of both justice and humanity.[103]

The list of ILO-sponsored conventions is long and impressive. It includes treaties on these topics[104]:

- medical examination of young persons
- weekly rest
- freedom of association and the right to organize
- work by women at night
- abolition of forced labor
- discrimination in employment
- protection against radiation
- hygiene in workplace and offices
- employment injury benefits
- disability, old-age, and survivors' benefits
- medical care and sickness benefits

---

103. August-1993, *supra* note 1, at pages 260–261.

104. This list is drawn from Jean Michel Serais, INTERNATIONAL LABOUR LAW (2005), at pages 305–306.

- minimum wages
- paid educational leave
- rural workers' organizations
- working environment (air pollution, noise, vibration)
- safety and health of dockworkers
- vocational rehabilitation
- protection against asbestos
- safety and health in construction work
- protection of indigenous and tribal peoples
- working conditions in hotels and restaurants
- part-time work
- safety and health in mines
- private employment agencies

International efforts on labor standards have not been confined to the ILO. Three key international legal instruments sponsored by the UN—the 1948 Declaration of Human Rights and the two 1966 International Covenants on Human Rights[105]—have also pronounced various rights and principles that all governments should protect. These include the right to safe and healthy working conditions, the right to a fair remuneration, the right to freedom of association in labor unions, and other rights. Several recent initiatives strive to ensure compliance with international labor standards, primarily in economically less developed countries. The USA, the EU, the WTO, and the World Bank are beginning to incorporate minimum labor rights and standards in trade pacts, investment treaties, and loans. Individual corporations and industry sectors have also begun incorporating labor rights and standards in corporate "codes of conduct".[106]

---

105. Universal Declaration of Human Rights, adopted by UN General Assembly Dec. 10, 1948; International Covenant on Civil and Political Rights, done at New York Dec. 16, 1966, entered into force Mar. 23, 1976, reprinted in 6 INTERNATIONAL LEGAL MATERIALS (1967) at page 368; International Covenant on Economic, Social, and Cultural Rights, done at New York Dec. 16, 1966; entered into force Jan. 3, 1976, reprinted in 6 INTERNATIONAL LEGAL MATERIALS (1967) at page 360.

106. See Jessica Learmond-Criqui, *Coordinating Crossborder Employment Law Projects, in* INTERNATIONAL EMPLOYMENT LAW: THE MULTINATIONAL EMPLOYER

Further Readings on Labor Law

(in addition to the sources cited in footnotes in this section)

International Labour Law (2005), by Jean-Michel Servais

International Labor and Employment Law (2006), edited by Philip M Berkowitz and Thomas Müller-Bonanni (giving legal details for thirteen countries around the world)

Comparative Labour Law and Industrial Relations in Industrialized Market Economies (2004), edited by Roger Blanpain

Labor Law in a Nutshell (Fourth Edition, 2000), by Douglas L. Leslie

Labor Relations in the Public Sector: Selected State and Federal Statutes (1994 Edition), by Harry T. Edwards, R. Theodore Clark, Jr., and Charles B. Craver

Labor Legislation and Public Policy: A Contemporary History (1993), by Paul Davies and Mark Freedland

Federal Law of Employment Discrimination in a Nutshell (Fourth Edition, 1999), by Mack A. Player

International Encyclopaedia for Labour Law and Industrial Relations (2001), edited by Roger Blanpain

International Employment Law: The Multinational Employer and the Global Workforce (1999), edited by Christian T. Campbell and Donald C. Dowling, Jr.

International Labour Conventions and Recommendations, 1919–1995 (1996), by International Labour Organization

III.B. Natural Resources and Environmental Law

The title of this section warrants some attention. The term "*natural resources law*" has until recently (perhaps twenty or thirty years

---

AND THE GLOBAL WORKFORCE (Dennis Campbell et al., eds., 1999), at pages 23–25.

ago in many economically developed countries) referred mainly to the rights of various entities—owners of land, holders of permits, government agencies, the public at large—in the exploitation of natural resources such as minerals, forests, oil and gas, and fisheries. In many countries, especially those rich in such resources, one or more separate laws were enacted long ago to deal with each such issue. At the international level, a general trend developed toward a strong assertion of national sovereignty over natural resources.

The term "*environmental law*", and the interest in environmental protection, is more recent. Environmental law has become popular (to different degrees in various countries) over the past twenty to thirty years because of a perception that economic development is producing pollutants that can damage human health and the ecological balance of a region, or indeed of the entire earth. The early emphasis on pollution has more recently expanded to include a broader concern for environmental protection more generally, including the preservation of biological diversity and the pursuit of development policies that are environmentally sustainable over many generations.

In fact, that notion of environmental sustainability has now become part of the view held by many people about how natural resources are to be developed and used. This view is often captured by the term "sustainable development". That term reflects the fact that few people in today's world would propose that natural resources should be used for short-term gain with callous disregard for long-term environmental effects; and few people would suggest that the level of environmental protection should be so high as to forbid the prudent use of natural resources to meet the needs of today.

Therefore, although the two terms that combine to create the title of this section—"natural resources law" and "environmental law"—have different and seemingly contradictory origins, with the first focusing more on exploitation and the other focusing more on protection and preservation, they are most properly seen today in tandem. Indeed, most highly developed national legal systems, as well as the international legal system, now conceive of a single topic—environmental law—that has two related elements: (i) law regarding the development and use of natural resources and (ii) environmental protection, including biological diversity, pollution control, and improvement of the human environment.

This understanding underlies many of the international rules that have developed in this area in recent years. The most important international conventions, declarations, and resolutions adopted under the auspices of the UN that focus on natural resources and environmental law include the following.[107]

- The 1972 Stockholm Declaration on the Human Environment articulates the human right to a decent environment and the sovereign right of nations (i) to exploit their own resources, but (ii) to ensure that their activities do not cause damage to other nations' environments.
- The 1991 Convention on Environmental Impact Assessment in a Transboundary Context (called the "Espoo Convention" because it was concluded in Espoo, Finland) is the only multilateral agreement on environmental impact assessment. It establishes a general framework for collaboration and certain procedural requirements among nations who undertake proposed projects, plans, and programs that are likely to pose significant adverse international environmental impacts.
- The 1992 Rio Declaration articulates the relationships between environmental protection and economic development.
- The 1998 Convention on Access to Information, Public Participation in Decision-Making and Access to Justice in Environmental Matters (called the Århus Convention for the city in Denmark where it was concluded) is the only multilateral environmental law treaty to provide specific procedural environmental rights, including rights of access to information, public participation in decision-making, and access to justice in environmental matters.
- The 2002 Johannesburg Declaration and the Plan of Implementation, which together articulate political commitments on

---

107. For details on these, see Key Materials in International Environmental Law (Phillippe Cullet & Alix Gowlland-Gualtieri, eds., 2004).

sustainable development and encourage the implementation of existing environmental commitments on poverty eradication, sustainable production and consumption, water and sanitation, and energy and chemicals.

III.B.1. Ownership and Exploitation of Natural Resources

A preliminary issue relates to *ownership and authority*. Typically, some natural resources are owned by the state and some by private parties. In many countries, for example, fisheries and at least some forests are owned by the state, which operates a permit system under which private enterprises are authorized to exploit the resources. Other resources are held by private sector entities, with exploitation regulated more or less strictly by the government. In many countries the rules permitting private sector entities to hold substantial interests over natural resources expressly exclude foreign investors. The particular details of ownership—public sector versus private sector, national versus foreigner—vary depending on the circumstances of a country, the nature of its resources, the domestic capacity for exploiting those resources, and so forth.

Related to the issue of ownership is the issue of *national development policy*. Where a high value is placed on exploiting natural resources in order to earn revenues, the government might provide incentives for exploitation. For example, if the government considers that fisheries stocks in a country's territorial waters or Exclusive Economic Zone are substantially under-utilized, the government might impose very low fisheries licensing fees, or perhaps even provide subsidies (especially to nationals of the country) to urge the better use of such resources. In the context of timber reserves, the government might allow long-term ownership interests to be held by private parties, even foreign persons, to spur commercial development of those reserves. On the other hand, where a government wishes to restrict such exploitation and development, it might tend to centralize more ownership in the public, protecting the resources through national preserves and parks.

III.B.2. Specific Regimes for Specific Resources

It is difficult to generalize about the legal rules governing the exploitation of particular types of natural resources. Each country's laws are different. However, some of the common issues that those laws typically must address are as follows:

for exploitation of mineral resources and oil and gas reserves ...

- How can an appropriate balance be struck between (i) the incentive to locate such resources and reserves (which usually require extensive prospecting and therefore many false starts) and (ii) the need to guard against both environmental destruction and violent controversies over claims to discovery?
- What is the relationship between ownership rights over the surface of an area and the rights in mineral resources or oil and gas reserves located beneath the surface—does one lead to the other, or are they always to be divided?
- If minerals have been discovered and mining has commenced, what are the limits—in time, in distance, and in types of minerals—to which an ownership claim or mining permit will extend?
- What methods and techniques will be permitted for the extraction and processing of the minerals or the oil and gas?
- If such extraction and processing involves the use of toxic materials, how will the waste products be managed and disposed of?
- Should certain areas or regions be "off-limits" to extraction entirely, in order to protect and preserve the natural habitat, indigenous cultures, or wilderness areas?
- What financial terms—royalties, purchase price, permit fees, etc.—are appropriate, and what procedures or agencies are established to set those terms and to deal with other related administrative matters?

for exploitation of timber resources ...

(in addition to some issues already raised above)
- What arrangements are to be made for access to timber resources, and especially for damage to surrounding areas (including erosion and runoff)?

- What limitations will be placed on timber companies regarding the selection of trees or sectors to be cut, and what requirements will be imposed on them to plant new trees on the lands they have cleared?
- In what other ways is the renewable nature of timber resources to be preserved, and what persons or institutions will have influence over these issues?
- What provisions will be or must be made for "multiple use" of forested areas—not only for such uses as inter-cropping or livestock management but also for purposes of recreation or wilderness preservation, or for protecting indigenous cultures?

for exploitation of water resources ...

(in addition to some issues already raised)
- What is the system for allocating water rights—for example, does the law recognize riparian rights limiting the use by upstream users of water resources, and if so, what obligations are there to maintain minimum flow and quality of water for various uses by others?
- What rights and obligations attach to water tables underlying surface water resources, and in particular what rates of exploitation are acceptable to avoid exhaustion, salinization, or pollution of groundwater?

for exploitation of fisheries resources ...

(in addition to some issues already raised)
- What balance of uses is to be maintained between fishing, navigation, recreation, and other purposes, and what rules on fishing vessels (marking, safety, operation, etc.) does that balance impose?
- What treaty obligations apply to the fishing or navigation by other countries or their nationals in various zones of the sea surrounding the country, including international passages and archipelagic seas?
- What measures can or must the coastal state take to protect marine mammals and highly migratory species, as well as to protect coral and other living resources of the sea?

III.B.3. Pollution Control and Remedies

As indicated above, pollution was an early topic of attention in the area of environmental law. It is still the most highly developed aspect of environmental law in many countries. Pollution control laws can operate in two different and complementary ways: (i) to provide for legal remedies (for example, compensation) after the pollution has already occurred; and more recently (ii) to impose a wide variety of requirements designed to prevent the occurrence of environmental harm in the first place. (The legal measures discussed in the next sub-section—environmental assessment and planning laws—typically operate only in the second of these ways.)

Pollution control laws often fall into the following categories:

- *air pollution* laws, which often establish ambient air quality standards (specifying how much of a particular pollutant is permitted in the air), methods of maintaining those standards, source standards (specifying how much of a particular pollutant one factory is permitted to emit), and prohibitions on the emission of certain especially hazardous pollutants;
- *water pollution* laws, which typically focus on effluent (discharge) limitations, requirements for treatment of discharged or run-off water, water quality standards, and thermal pollution;
- *solid waste pollution* laws, which include provisions on the treatment, storage, and disposal of hazardous waste;
- *"cleanup"* laws allocating legal liability for the cost of repairing pollution damage, sometimes by emphasizing the "polluter pays principle" and sometimes by establishing funds contributed to by business entities engaged in specified operations;
- *pesticide licensing and certification* laws, which permit certain chemicals to be used only by trained persons and subject to strict limitations;
- *labeling requirements*, which disclose and warn against health and environmental hazards associated with certain products;
- *reporting requirements* that force companies to publicize their compliance (or their non-compliance) with environmental laws and regulations; and

- *"cap-and-trade"* laws, which permit companies to buy and sell certain pollution allowances as part of a system designed to reduce the aggregate amount of pollution.

One of the most aggressive legal initiatives regarding some of the types of pollution control referred to in the above list comes out of the European Commission. Referred to as the "REACH" ("Registration, Evaluation, and Authorization of Chemicals") program, this initiative took effect in June 2007. It seeks (i) to ensure testing for long-established chemicals that have never been tested, (ii) to shift the burden of proof from the government to producers and importers of chemicals, and (iii) to phase out the use of high-concern substances and to replace them with safer alternatives. The REACH program requires chemical producers to provide information on the toxicity of many of the chemicals they use, and it also requires special government authorization before a company could use certain chemicals.

III.B.4. Environmental Assessment and Planning

In order to ensure that environmental factors are considered early in the process of economic development operations—including mining, fishing, and other forms of extraction, but also road construction, land clearing, town planning, and so forth—many countries' laws now require environmental assessment and planning. The *environmental assessment* procedure is designed to identify, and quantify if possible, the environmental damage (or in some cases environmental enhancement) that can reasonably be expected from such development and exploitation activities. Thus, instead of making decisions on proposals to engage in such activities based only on financial or economic calculations, persons responsible for making the decisions must also take into account environmental costs. Those costs are often difficult to quantify, of course, but the process of examining them and including them in the decisional process forces a recognition of the fact that persons engaged in the development and exploitation activity should not be permitted to realize short-term gain by imposing long-term (environmental) costs on the rest of the community—or on a part of the community such as indigenous peoples.

Environmental planning is somewhat different. Instead of being reactive—environmental assessment requirements, after all, are usually triggered only by a proposed action of some sort—environmental planning is *anticipatory* in nature. It involves the inclusion of environmental factors in the long-term development plans and policy of a community or country.

Of these two related methods of environmental protection, environmental assessment is now widely accepted. All the major economic development assistance agencies, such as the World Bank and the Asian Development Bank, require rigorous environmental impact assessments to be conducted in any projects they support that are identified (through a detailed "screening" process) as having any significant environmental implications. Indeed, the European Bank for Reconstruction and Development has a specific "environmental mandate" set forth in its charter regarding environmental protection. Most national laws now require environmental impact assessments domestically as well.

Further Readings on Natural Resources and Environmental Law

(in addition to the sources cited in footnotes in this section)

Hornbook on The Law of Oil and Gas (Third Edition, 1992), by Richard W. Hemingway

Modern Public Land Law in a Nutshell (Third Edition, 2006), by Robert L. Glicksman and George Cameron Coggins

Energy and Natural Resources Law in a Nutshell (1992), by Jan G. Laitos and Joseph P. Tomain

Environmental Protection: Law and Policy (Fifth Edition, 2007), by Robert L. Glicksman, David L. Markell, William W. Buzbee, Daniel R. Mandelker, and A. Dan Tarlock

Environmental Regulations: Law, Science, and Policy (Fifth Edition, 2006), by Robert V. Percival, Alan Miller, Christopher H. Schroeder, and James P. Leape

A Manual of Nature Conservation Law (1995), by Michael Fry

Environmental Regulation and Economic Growth (1995), edited by A.E. Boyle

International Law and the Environment (2002), by Patricia W. Birnie and Alan E. Boyle

Environmental and Planning Law (January 1995), by Yvonne Scannell

Selected Environmental Law Statutes—1996–97 (1996)

Environmental Law in a Nutshell (Sixth Edition, 2004), by Roger W. Findley and Daniel A. Farber

Hornbook on Environmental Law (1995 Edition), by William H. Rodgers

Environmental Law (four volumes, updated annually), by William H. Rodgers

Manual of European Environmental Law (1997 Edition), by Alexandre Charles Kiss and Dinah Shelton

Environmental Impact Assessment (EIA)—Cutting Edge for the 21st Century (1995 Edition), by Alan Gilpin

Basic Documents on International Law and the Environment (1996 Edition), collected by Alan Boyle and Patricia Birnie

III.C. Product Liability and Consumer Protection

Product liability law can be seen as a particular aspect—an especially important aspect, from the perspective of a business entity—of consumer protection law. The following paragraphs focus first on product liability and then turn to a more general survey of consumer protection law.

III.C.1. Product Liability

A legal topic of growing significance to business entities concerns their *liability for injuries* resulting from the use of the products they manufacture or sell. Assume, for example, that a company operating out of Mumbai manufactures televisions for sale in Africa, Japan, Europe, and the USA. If several of those televisions are defective and explode, causing serious injury to the persons who ultimately purchased and used the televisions, can the Mumbai-based company be judged liable for those injuries and be required to pay damages?

The answer differs from one legal system to another. In Europe and the USA, the answer is almost surely yes—the company could face enormous financial liability. The trend in many countries around the world over the past few decades has been toward providing more and more protection to consumers by placing more and more liability on the manufacturers or sellers of consumer products.

Traditionally, these issues were typically handled under normal rules of the *law of obligations*, divided in some systems (especially common-law systems) between contract obligations and tort obligations. *Note:* The term "tort" as used in common law countries may be defined generally as a wrongful act, outside the context of a contractual relationship, by which one person causes some injury to another person, thereby triggering an obligation to compensate the injured person. The notion of "tort" is closely related to the notion of "delict" as used in many civil law countries.

Under the first of these—contract obligations—the predominant rule was stated in the Latin phrase *caveat emptor*, which means "let the buyer beware!" In other words, the seller of goods generally was not liable for any problems in the goods, or injury they caused, unless a specific provision in the contract imposed that liability on the seller. Instead, the buyer was responsible for inspecting the goods for defects or for suitability to the purpose he or she had in mind for those goods. Today, according to one American writer, the rules in the USA "have been reversed almost completely; the rule might more accurately be described as *caveat vendor*—let the seller beware! ... Liability has changed from its basis in the parties' contract to a set of social rules imposed by the courts and the legislatures."[108] The USA is not alone in this respect. Other countries have witnessed similar developments.

---

108. Cameron, *supra* note 1, at page 458.

A related development has appeared in the area of tort obligations. In most legal systems people have a duty to exercise ordinary care in conducting their affairs, so as to avoid undue injury or damage to other people or their property. If, through negligence, a person violates that duty—that is, commits a tort, then compensation is due. In other words, persons are held liable for the results of their carelessness and disregard of the health, safety, or property of others. On that basis, if a manufacturer of a product acts negligently in making it and thereby injures or endangers a consumer, compensation is due. This rule is commonplace. In some legal systems, however, the responsibility of a manufacturer for a product it makes now extends much further: a manufacturer can be liable to pay compensation for any injury, even if there was no negligence involved at all. Where this "strict liability" or "absolute liability" approach is taken, it sometimes applies only to specific kinds of products—those that are considered to be inherently dangerous. Of course, it might be difficult to know in advance whether a product is "inherently dangerous".

The three bases of liability referred to above—contract, negligence, and "strict liability"—appear in different contexts in different legal systems. According to one author, "[m]ost states (including Japan and most of the states of the developing world) use only the first two of these. The common law countries (i.e., the USA and the British commonwealth countries) use all three. The European Community now relies principally on the last" of those three bases of liability.[109]

Another topic falling within the area of product liability relates to *defenses*—arguments that can be raised by a business entity that has been accused of being liable for injury or damage as a result of products it made or sold. These also vary from market to market (that is, from one legal system to another), but they can be classified as follows:

- defenses claiming that the injured consumer was in fact the primary cause of the injury. This is sometimes referred to as "*con-*

---

109. August-1993, *supra* note 1, at page 177. For a survey of product liability laws in European and some non-European countries, see Dennis Campbell and Christian T. Campbell, INTERNATIONAL PRODUCT LIABILITY (Lloyd's of London Press, 1993).

tributory negligence", because the consumer contributed, by his or her own negligence, to the injury. This can sometimes serve as a complete defense or can sometimes serve to lessen the compensation that a business entity has to pay.

- defenses claiming that the injured consumer was fully aware of the risks involved in using the product and did so anyway. This *"assumption of risk"* argument might not apply if the consumer in fact had no choice but to use the product (because of unequal bargaining power) and if the product could have been made safer.

- defenses claiming that the state of *scientific or technical knowledge* at the time the product was made or distributed was not advanced enough to permit a defect to be discovered.

- defenses claiming that adequate *warnings or disclaimers* were provided to alert the consumer of the risks involved in using the product and the restricted responsibility that the maker or seller of the product was accepting.

In sum, business entities (especially manufacturers) need to be aware of the rules relating to product liability, negligence, strict or absolute liability, and other possible grounds on which they might be found financially responsible for injury or damage that results from the use of products they make or sell. Indeed, in some markets a business entity might have liability for injury or damage even if it cannot be proven that the injury or damage resulted from the use of that business entity's products; as long as the business entity is the producer of *some* of the articles of a particular type in that market, and as long as the injury or damage resulted from use of that type of article, all producers might share liability. The risks of such liability must be taken into account in a decision whether or not to sell goods into a particular market.

III.C.2. Consumer Protection

Product liability is an especially important aspect of consumer protection law generally. In many legal systems, governments are increasingly involved in a variety of efforts to protect consumers. For example, in October 2001, the European Commission issued a "Green Paper" on consumer protection, which summarized the European Union's consumer protection objectives but recognized that many of the objectives had yet to be fully achieved in its member nations. In both Canada and the USA, laws on consumer protection are enacted by legislatures at the provincial (or state) level as well as at the federal level. Government agencies also adopt rules regulating consumer protection.[110] This trend toward increasing government involvement in consumer protection might reflect in part the globalization of the world economy; increasingly more consumer transactions are conducted with business entities that are not personally known to the consumers, and many of those business entities have vastly greater bargaining power than the consumers do.

A list of *efforts at consumer protection* would include the following:

- laws imposing "fairness" requirements on *standard-form contracts*. If George Roth hires a car from a car-rental company at Heathrow (London) international airport, he has virtually no bargaining power regarding the terms of that contract. In recognition of that fact, and to guard against an unfairly one-sided contract being imposed by the car-rental company, statutory rules or government agency regulations might require that the contract include a variety of provisions to protect George Roth—such as a promise by the company to provide a replacement automobile if the one first given to George Roth is defective, or a guarantee that disputes or complaints can be brought before a government agency in the United Kingdom.

- laws prohibiting *deception and fraud* in consumer transactions. The term "deception" would carry different specific meanings in different legal systems, of course, but in many cases the term would apply to a practice that is likely to mislead consumers

---

110. See William T. Vukowich, CONSUMER PROTECTION IN THE 21ST CENTURY (2002), at pages 94–100.

who are acting reasonably (that is, who are not so gullible as to believe absolutely everything they read or hear) and who are materially injured as a result.[111] By contrast, "fraud" is typically more serious and more difficult to establish. For example, in English and American common law, fraud consisted of five elements: a false representation; the defendant's intentional making of that false representation, expecting reliance; the defendant's knowledge of the falsity of the representation; reliance on that false representation by the plaintiff; and injury to the plaintiff as a result of that reliance.[112]

• laws requiring *disclosure of product information* to consumers. These might stipulate that companies engaged in financial products and services—banking, insurance, and the like—provide specified types of information about the safety or liquidity of financial products they sell, or about the full range of fees applicable to certain types of services. Other such laws might require labeling of the ingredients included in food products, or providing instructions and warnings with kitchen appliances, or including a written warning of the health hazards of cigarette smoking.

• laws *prohibiting specified sales practices*. These might disallow, for example, a provision in an insurance contract stating that the insurance policy is automatically canceled if the insured person is even one day late in paying the premium. In the context of an appliance business, such laws might disallow a "cross-collateral" provision, under which payments that a consumer makes over time on one appliance would be collateralized by a long list of items already purchased from that same appliance business.

• laws guaranteeing consumers *access to financial information* relating to business or themselves. These might include require-

---

111. This description of elements of "deception" is drawn from the *Consumer Protection Handbook* issued in 2004 by the American Bar Association Section on Antitrust Law, at page 6.

112. *Id.* at pages 7–8.

ments that a business make available to consumers financial and other information about the business, to assist the consumer in deciding whether to enter into a transaction with that entity or to buy one of its products. Such laws might also require that consumers have access to information kept about them by business or government entities regarding personal finances.

Lastly, consumer protection could also be seen as including certain *rules of court*. Increasingly, courts in various countries are accepting cases brought jointly by a large number of individual claimants against a particular business entity. These "representative actions" or "class actions" or "mass actions"—the terminology differs depending on the legal system—are important from the perspective of the business entity, of course, because they tend to overcome the natural advantage that such an entity has in such cases.

Further Readings on Product Liability and Consumer Protection

(in addition to the sources cited in footnotes in this section)

Guide to Product Liability in Asia-Pacific (1999 Edition), edited by Jocelyn Kellam

Guide to Product Liability in Europe: The New Strict Product Liability Laws, Pre-Existing Remedies, Procedure and Costs in the European Free Trade Association (1994), by William C. Hoffman and Susanne Hill-Arning

International Product Liability (1993), edited by Dennis Campbell and Christian T. Campbell

International Consumer Protection (1995), edited by Dennis Campbell

South American Consumer Protection Laws (1996), by David B. Jaffe and Robert G. Vaughn

Commercial and Consumer Law: National and International Dimensions (1993), edited by Ross Cranston and Roy Goode

Consumer Law—Nutshell (2000), by Sandra Silberstein

III.D. Tax Law

Business decisions are made predominantly on the basis of profit considerations. One of the key determinants of a business entity's profits is the extent to which the entity has to pay taxes to the government—or perhaps to several governments, if the business entity is operating in more than one country.

Obviously, an understanding of tax law is crucial to the success of business organizations. And an understanding of tax law requires not only knowing about calculating taxes but also knowing about the underlying policies on which a country's tax system rests. In many countries, one main goal of the tax system is *tax-neutrality*, which calls for tax rules that neither discourage nor encourage any particular activity; according to this way of thinking, business decisions should be made for non-tax reasons.[113] Tax neutrality includes the following three characteristics:

- capital-export neutrality—this means that a business entity's choice between investing at home or abroad should not be influenced by taxation.
- capital-import neutrality—otherwise known as foreign or competitive neutrality, this means that all business entities conducting operations or transactions in a particular market, regardless of whether those business entities are domestic or foreign, should be taxed at the same rate.
- national neutrality—this means that returns on capital are shared between the business entity and the national treasury, regardless of whether the capital is invested in the business entity's "home" nation or abroad.[114]

Some countries, including the USA, have tax laws that reflect (imperfectly) these three characteristics, but many countries have tax laws that reflect other priorities. In this way, and many other ways as well, tax laws differ substantially from one country to another.

---

113. See Richard L. Doernberg, INTERNATIONAL TAXATION IN A NUTSHELL (6th ed. 2004), at pages 3–5.

114. *Id.*

Another difference is that taxes can come in many forms. One of the most common types is the income tax. It will be discussed first in the paragraphs that follow, and then attention will turn briefly to sales taxes, VAT taxes, and other forms of taxation.

III.D.1. Income Tax

A key source of revenue for most governments is the income tax. In many cases, the income tax takes the form of what has been termed a "*global progressive tax*". It is global in the sense that all sources of income are subject to the same tax rates. This is the opposite of a system in which different rates apply to different economic sectors. The purposes of such differentiation among sectors would be to encourage investment in particular sectors and to discourage it (relatively speaking) in other sectors. A "global progressive tax" is progressive in the sense that it imposes higher tax rates on higher levels of income.

According to a recent survey of 100 countries, about one-third of them applied a global form of income tax (as described above) to *companies* operating in their territory, and about 90 of them imposed a similar tax on *individuals* residing in their territory. Some of those countries elaborated on the global form of income tax by fixing different rates for a few specific industries, or for companies that are partially or wholly foreign-owned, or for companies having shares that are publicly-traded. According to the same survey, about one-third of the countries surveyed used progressive tax rates for companies, often ranging from 20% to 40%. The others use flat rates, but sometimes (as noted above) with different rates for a few specific industries.

With tax rates that high, it becomes very important to know what base amount is being used to represent a company's **taxable income**. In other words, what is the amount that a tax rate of, say, 30% will be multiplied by in order to calculate the total amount of tax owed? Two major issues arise in this regard.

The first issue relating to a determination of taxable income concerns **which of several approaches** a tax system uses—the nationality of the taxpayer, the residence of the taxpayer, the source of the taxpayer's income, or some combination of the three. One reference book on international taxation[115] offers the following definitions:

- *Nationality Principle*: A state may tax the worldwide income of its citizens or nationals, no matter where they may reside. (The USA follows this approach for federal income tax.)
- *Residency Principle*: A state may tax the worldwide income of persons who are legally residing within its territory. (Different states use different criteria in determining residence of individuals, including (i) length of time within the territory, (ii) subjective intent to remain in residence, and (iii) declaration by the person of an intent to stay. For companies, residence is usually determined by (i) where the company was organized or (ii) where the company is managed and controlled.)
- *Source Principle*: A state may tax income derived from sources within its territory, and thus exempt from taxation income derived from outside sources. (Income that is taxed under this principle usually includes (i) income derived from property located within the country, such as income in the form of dividends on equity shares in a company, (ii) income derived from any trade or profession carried on within the country, such as income from agricultural activity or mining, and (iii) income derived from employment carried on within the country.)

The second major issue relating to a determination of income concerns the *method of calculation* to be used. The two main methods are (i) the income statement method and (ii) the balance sheet method. The difference between an income statement and a balance sheet was discussed above in section D of Chapter I. The USA, the United Kingdom, Canada, and some other countries use the *income statement method*. That is, income is determined after offsetting allowable losses and deductions from all revenues received during an

---

115. This formulation, as well as some other material in the following paragraphs, is drawn from chapter 13 of August-1993, *supra* note 1. August attributes these definitions to J.D.R. Adams and J. Whaley, THE INTERNATIONAL TAX-ATION OF MULTINATIONAL ENTERPRISES IN DEVELOPED COUNTRIES (1977). Similar definitions appear also in Doernberg, *supra* note 113, at pages 7–10.

accounting period. Most other countries in the world use the *balance sheet method*, in which income is determined by calculating the difference between the net worth of a business entity at the beginning of an accounting period and its net worth at the end of that period.

For a company operating in two different countries, the prospect of *double taxation* becomes important. Assume, for example, that a company manufacturing furniture in Atlanta operates a sales office in Mexico, where most of the furniture is sold. If both the Mexican and the US tax systems would apply to the company, it will want to avoid having to pay tax twice on the same income (arising from the sale of the furniture). Fortunately for the company, it is now the practice in most countries to provide relief from such double taxation. That relief can take several different forms—tax credits, tax exemptions, tax deductions—and these are designed to reduce or eliminate the taxes owed in one of the two countries.

In many cases the relief is guaranteed by way of a *tax treaty* between the two countries involved. Tax treaties go back at least to the 1920s, when the League of Nations sponsored the drafting of several model tax treaties. Other model tax treaties have been prepared by the Organisation for Economic Cooperation and Development ("OECD") and the UN. Some of the principal topics addressed in these models, and in tax treaties based on them, are (i) the taxes and persons covered by the treaty, (ii) whether the nationality principle, the residency principle, or the source principle (as described above) is to be used, and (iii) provisions for avoiding double taxation.

A final noteworthy issue relating to income taxes is this: should corporate income—that is, income earned by businesses that operate by way of a corporate structure with independent legal personality—be taxed? Debate over this issue swirls in many countries, and the question gets answered differently in different countries and at different times. Most countries do, in fact, now tax corporate income, but they give various answers to a secondary question: in taxing corporate income, what rates and what procedures should be used to protect investors against "double exposure" to taxation? An investor is said to suffer from "double exposure" in the sense that (i) he or she must pay taxes on dividends issued to the investor by the corporate entity and (ii) the overall profit of the corporate entity, and therefore the dividends it pays to the investor, are reduced as a result of the tax levied on the corporate entity itself.

III.D.2. Other Forms of Taxation

Income taxes are not the only source of government revenue, of course. Most countries have other forms of taxation as well. In some countries, these other forms of taxation are more important than the income tax.

There are, for example, many forms of what is sometimes called a *"turnover" tax*.[116] A turnover tax is one that is collected at a "turnover" time—the time a product (or in some cases a service) reaches a new stage in the production or distribution process. An example of a turnover tax is a sales tax charged whenever a product is turned over—that is, sold from one person to another. A sales tax typically takes the form of a percentage of the sales price. It represents a cumulative turnover tax because at each stage the purchase price includes an increasing amount of tax, because tax is being paid on tax.

Another form of turnover tax is the VAT—value added tax. It is "a tax on turnover whose payment is split between all the economic stages that it covers, in the sense that at each of the stages that a product passes through, the tax is levied on the value added to the product at that stage."[117] Unlike the sales tax, the VAT is not cumulative in effect; tax is being charged only on value added and not on the amounts of taxes imposed at earlier economic stages. Here is how one authority describes, by way of a simple illustration, the operation of a VAT:

> The basic principle of VAT is that it is a sales tax chargeable to the sellers of all output, with the proviso that in computing their liability firms may deduct any VAT that has been

---

116. This is the term used by August-1993, *supra* note 1, at pages 730–733.

117. This definition comes from work done in the European Economic Community, as appearing in *The EEC Reports on Tax Harmonization* (1963).

levied on inputs into their products. We can see how this works by considering a simple example with a standard rate of VAT of 15 per cent. Suppose a man discovers a block of iron which with the aid of a magic wand (provided free of charge) he turns into steel worth £100. Adding VAT at 15 per cent he sells this to a motor car firm for £115 [and pays the £15 VAT to the government tax authorities]. The [motor car] firm buys additional components which cost £500 to make and on which it is charged £75 VAT [by the seller of those components, which pays that £75 VAT to the tax authorities], and employs labour at a cost of £400. [The motor car firm] sells the car for £1,300, charging 15 per cent VAT [i.e., £195], to make up a total price to the purchaser of £1,495, and secures a profit of £300. The firm then must account to the [tax authorities] for the difference between the VAT levied on its outputs (£195) and the VAT charged on its inputs (£90) so that it makes a payment [to the tax authorities] of £105. This amounts to 15 per cent of the £700 of *value added* in the car factory—the difference between the values of inputs and outputs, made up of £400 of labour costs plus £300 profit.… At the same time as the VAT man receives the car firm's cheque for £105, he also gets £75 from the component manufacturer and £15 from the steel producer, so that in aggregate £195 (15 per cent of the value of the final output) is levied on the sequence of transactions involved in the production of the car.[118]

In addition to income taxes and turnover taxes, the other common forms of taxation imposed in various countries include (i) *documentary stamp taxes* for transfers of real estate or securities, (ii) *net worth taxes*, (iii) *excise taxes* on certain products, and (iv) *import and export taxes*. Import taxes (also called tariffs or duties) are widely used and are subject to the General Agreement on Tariffs and Trade dis-

---

118. J.A. King and M.A. King, THE BRITISH TAX SYSTEM (4th ed. 1986), at pages 132–133.

cussed in Chapter IV. Export taxes are less common, mainly because most countries want to encourage exports, not discourage them through taxation.

Further Readings on Tax Law

(in addition to the sources cited in footnotes in this section)

Hornbook on Corporate Income Taxation (Fifth Edition, 2001), by Douglas A. Kahn and Jeffrey S. Lehman

Black Letter on Federal Income Taxation (Sixth Edition, 2002), by David M. Hudson and Stephen A. Lind

Federal Income Taxation (Eleventh Edition, 2000), by William A. Klein and Joseph Bankman

EC Tax Law (1995), by Paul Farmer and Richard Lyal

International Tax Planning (1996), edited by Dennis Campbell

III.E. Protecting the Economy against Corruption and Terrorism

Several of the topics already covered above in this Chapter on the role of government in the economy emphasized the government's protective role—that is, the responsibility of the government to take action that will protect against activities that undermine the smooth functioning of the economy or that unfairly prey upon innocent parties. Labor law protects workers against improper treatment by more powerful business interests. Environmental law protects all citizens against the dishonesty or incompetence of some persons who would destroy important natural resources. Products liability law and consumer law protect against the underhanded tactics of some persons who sell goods or services that are dangerous or fraudulent.

This last section briefly discusses two other forms of improper activity that the government should protect against, in the interest of facilitating an economy that operates smoothly and fairly. The first of these is corruption, which includes in its most common form the bribery of public officials in order to gain special treatment that is undeserved. The second form of improper activity discussed below is terrorism, a topic that has recently gained much greater attention.

III.E.1. Anti-Corruption

Most forms of official corruption—that is, payments made to government officials in order to corrupt or distort their decisions, especially regarding the awarding of business contracts or the granting of business licenses—are usually both *inefficient and unfair.* An example will illustrate this fact. Assume that a government agency in Turkey plans to purchase two thousand new computers and associated software programs, and that two private companies, Company A and Company B, both submit bids to that agency in hopes of entering into a contract to supply the computers and software. Assume further that Company A offers a sales price of 700,000 Turkish lira and Company B offers a sales price of 800,000 Turkish lira for identical equipment. Lastly, assume that Company B secretly pays 15,000 Turkish lira to each of the three government officials primarily responsible for making the decision, in order to influence those officials so that they will award the contract to Company B. If the government officials yield to the temptation to take the bribe and award the contract to Company B, the contract will cost the government, and therefore the society as a whole, much more—nearly 15 percent more (800,000 lira instead of 700,000 lira)—than it would if the award of contract were conducted honestly. Moreover, of course, the bribery brings a result that is unfair to Company A, which did not offer a bribe, and that inappropriately rewards the three dishonest officials for their greed and breach of responsibility.

This basic fact, that corruption is typically both inefficient and unfair, has prompted many governments to take some *legal action against bribery.* In many countries, the effectiveness of that legal action is inconsistent because of several factors. For one thing, the salaries of government officials might be so low as to virtually force them to rely on private payments for their services. In addition, the social and economic ties between government officials and business managers might be so strong that special commissions or gifts or bribes or other forms of payment are regarded as simply part of the process by which business is conducted.

Some nations took an aggressive approach starting in the 1970s to outlaw the making of bribes and other corrupt payments. The USA, for example, enacted the Foreign Corrupt Practices Act in 1977 in response to disclosures that large USA-based companies had paid large bribes to foreign government officials in order to obtain or retain business. Recently, this approach has been taken also at the *international level*. In 1997, the Organization for Economic Cooperation and Development ("OECD") finalized a treaty on this subject. It is titled the Convention on Combating Bribery of Foreign Public Officials in International Business Transactions, and it sets forth the commitment of its participating states to impose effective criminal penalties on persons who offer or give any thing of value to a foreign public official in order to induce that official to award business to the person who makes such a payment. As of mid-2007, about 36 countries had become parties to that treaty.

III.E.2. Anti-Terrorism

Why does this book, which offers an introduction to general principles of business and economic law, include a subsection on terrorism and methods of combating terrorism? For two reasons. First, among the numerous reasons why a government would wish to suppress terrorist activities is a simple economic reason: *terrorist activities can be disastrous to an economy*. If terrorism threatens the peace and security of a population, economic activity is distorted or reduced. Productive economic activity, such as the building of commercial facilities or the manufacture and sale of consumer goods, might be converted to protective economic activity, such as increasing security measures. Normal investment can be driven away because of the uncertainty that terrorism brings.

A second reason why this book on economic law includes a discussion of terrorism is that one of the key ways of combating terrorism is through economic and financial means—by cutting off the methods by which terrorist activities are financed. As a former US foreign minister has expressed it, "terrorism is not a self-sustaining enterprise. It needs money and supplies to succeed."[119]

There is not yet an internationally-accepted *definition of terrorism*. Perhaps this lack of consensus reflects the fact that, as has widely been suggested, "one man's terrorist is another man's freedom fighter." However, the definitions that have been proposed thus far typically involve several factors: violence, innocent victims, political motivations, and non-state actors. For example, US statutory law defines terrorism as "premeditated, politically motivated violence perpetrated against noncombatant targets by sub-national groups or clandestine agents".[120] The aims of terrorism are often to disrupt normal life dramatically enough to destabilize a government or an economy (i) by forcing it to devote precious financial and other resources to increasing the protection of civilians against such attacks and (ii) by driving away commerce (including, for example, tourist trade), discouraging investment, and undermining confidence in the country's economic and financial institutions.

Some observers have asserted that "[t]he fight against terrorism requires a concerted and multifaceted strategy at both the domestic and international level and should involve military, economic, diplomatic, and legal methods."[121] For our purposes, it is most important to see how government authorities have turned to *financial measures* to fight terrorism. Terrorist organizations are financed in many ways, both legal and illegal. These include (i) criminal activity by the organizations themselves (such as dealing in drugs and conducting fraudulent transactions), (ii) funding by state entities (several countries have been accused of providing financial support for terrorists),

---

119. Gregory C. Clark, *History Repeating Itself: The [D]evolution of Recent British and American Antiterrorist Legislation*, 27 FORDHAM URBAN LAW JOURNAL (1999), at pages 247, 269 (quoting former US Secretary of State Madeleine Albright).

120. United States Code, Title 22, Section 2656f(d)(2).

121. See Van Krieken, TERRORISM AND THE INTERNATIONAL LEGAL ORDER (2002), at page 1.

(iii) popular support by way of private donations of money, (iv) earnings on investments owned by the organization, and (v) some form of taxation conducted by the organization.[122]

Governments can take three basic approaches to counter these various methods of terrorist financing. One approach is to strengthen the *regulations governing financial institutions*, in order to force them to help law enforcement officials monitor large transactions that might be involved in financing terrorist activities. For example, banks can be required to report large or suspicious transfers of funds or currency transactions, especially those that might reflect efforts to "launder" illegally obtained funds. (See the brief discussion of money-laundering in subsection C.3. of Chapter II, above.)

A second approach to combating terrorism is to *criminalize the concealment of illegally obtained funds* and the raising of illegal funds. Any such funds that law enforcement officials discover may be seized. A third approach is to *criminalize the making of private contributions* to terrorist organizations. For example, legislation in both the USA and the United Kingdom makes it illegal to provide financial or practical support to certain designated organizations that are known or thought to have links to terrorists or terrorist activities.[123] Sometimes such laws do more than simply criminalize contributions to the terrorist factions of organizations; they also extend to the humanitarian activities of such organizations, so that financial contributions to peaceful and legal branches of organizations are also illegal if the organization has any branch that engages in terrorist activity. The restrictions that such laws impose are sometimes challenged as violating the human rights of free speech and free association.

National anti-terrorism laws are only as effective as the government's ability and determination to enforce them. One key issue in this regard, especially when foreign-based terrorism is involved, concerns *jurisdiction*: under what circumstances can the courts of one

---

122. For a discussion of these and other methods by which terrorist activities are financed, see Stephen C. Warneck, *A Preemptive Strike: Using RICO and the AEDPA to Attack the Financial Strength of International Terrorist Organizations*, 78 BOSTON UNIVERSITY LAW REVIEW (1998), at pages 177, 184–187.

123. Clark, *supra* note 119, at pages 256, 268.

country exercise jurisdiction over persons who are not citizens or residents of that country? This issue is under debate now, as it can represent a clash between (i) principles of international law regarding sovereignty of independent states and (ii) the need to combat terrorism wherever it is based.

In the aftermath of recent terrorist attacks—for example, those in the USA in September 2001 and in London in July 2005—increased *international cooperation* will probably continue to emerge in the fight against terrorism. Even before that point in time, however, considerable headway had been made, including the preparation of several treaties. Two of those treaties were adopted by the UN General Assembly in the late 1990s: the International Convention for the Suppression of Terrorist Bombings (1997) and the International Convention for the Suppression of the Financing of Terrorism (1999).[124]

Further Readings on Protecting against Corruption and Terrorism

(in addition to the sources cited in footnotes in this section)

Corruption and the Global Economy (1997), edited by Kimberly Ann Elliot

"The Foreign Corrupt Practices Act", appearing in Business Laws, Inc., *Corporate Counsel's Guide to Laws of International Trade—Executive Legal Summary No. 5* (2000)

see the website of the Organization for Economic Cooperation and Development (www.oecd.org)

Terrorism and the International Legal Order (2002), by Peter J. van Krieken

---

124. The first of these entered into force in May 2001 and as of mid 2007 had 148 parties. The second one entered into force in April 2002 and as of mid 2007 had 154 parties. For the text and status of these treaties, see the information about terrorism conventions on the UN website, at www.un.org. See also John W. Head, *Essay: The United States and International Law after September 11*, 11 KANSAS JOURNAL OF LAW AND PUBLIC POLICY (2001), at pages 1, 15 (note 29).

Chapter IV

Relations with Other Economies

A book explaining the principles of business and economic law would be incomplete without an account of rules that focus specifically on *international* relations. Why? Because even though (as noted above) most economic law is national law, the increasing pace of globalization has prompted the development of many rules and institutions outside the parameters of the nation-state. These multilateral sets of rules relating to economic relations are gradually playing a larger and larger role in the lives of all people—not just those who live in the wealthier countries of the world and who operate big companies but people all over the world, especially consumers and those who operate and work in small businesses. It is for those reasons that we now turn to several subjects relating to international business and economic law.

IV.A. International Business Transactions in General

Used broadly, the term "international business transactions" encompasses all economic transactions or relations in which not all of the involved parties are from the same country. Other similar terms include "transnational business", "cross-border transactions", and "global economic relations". The key element in all these is the fact that more than one nationality is involved. This is significant because most rules of law, including rules of economic law, have traditionally been national in scope and source. If a business entity engages in international business activity, as distinct from domestic business activity (all within one nation's borders), that business entity will need to consider and abide by the rules of economic law applicable in the other countries of operation.

Therefore, much of the law of international business transactions involves issues of how various nations' laws conflict or overlap with each other. More recently, most countries in the world have taken steps to reduce the conflict or overlap by creating sets of "multilateral" rules of economic law — that is, rules that transcend national borders and that apply equally in all participating countries. Some of these rules reflect economic theories that favor the free trading of goods and services across national borders.

International business transactions may, for purposes of discussion, be classified into three parts: (1) *sales of goods across borders*; (2) *licensing production abroad*; and (3) *foreign direct investment*. The distinctions between the three parts can be illustrated by an example. Assume a company named Bubba Company ("Bubba") manufactures automobiles in Seattle. If Bubba is successful in selling its Bubcar automobiles in the USA, it might decide to expand into other markets outside the USA. In other words, it might believe that its manufacturing experience and the design of its Bubcar automobiles would make them attractive to buyers in other countries. An obvious way that Bubba could expand its operations to overseas markets would be to export some of the Bubcar automobiles it manufactures in Seattle to buyers in the Philippines or Europe. That would be a *sale of goods across borders*, the first type of transaction mentioned above.

A second type of international transaction is the *licensing of production abroad*. In the example offered above, Bubba might enter into a licensing contract with a company in the Philippines, named Catuncan Company. Under that licensing contract, Catuncan Company would manufacture automobiles using the technology that Bubba had developed (designs, special machinery, production techniques, and so forth) and would put the Bubba name on the cars and sell them in the Philippines and Japan. For the right to use that technology and the Bubba name, and to sell the automobiles in the Philippines and Japan, Catuncan Company would be required under the licensing contract to pay money to Bubba — perhaps a fixed amount of money each year plus a "royalty" of a certain amount for each automobile produced under those arrangements. This is a licensing transaction.

A third type of international business transaction is *foreign direct investment*. Bubba might decide that it would like to open its own manufacturing plant in the Philippines. Instead of entering into a contract with Catuncan Company, Bubba could buy or lease some land and buildings near Manila, either in its own name or by establishing a subsidiary under the laws of the Philippines, and then handle all of the manufacturing and selling of Bubcar automobiles itself. An advantage to Bubba in doing this is that Bubba would be receiving the profits from the sales instead of just fees and royalties from Catuncan Company as in a licensing arrangement. The disadvantage to Bubba, of course, is that now Bubba would bear all the risk of loss and would have the responsibility for managing all the legal and operational affairs of the plant in a foreign country.

For these and many other reasons, Bubba might decide to conduct its foreign direct investment by means of a *joint venture*. A joint venture is a joint undertaking by two existing businesses in which they share resources, profits, losses, responsibilities, liabilities, control, and management.[125]

Some of the forms of international business transactions mentioned above are also known as *strategic alliances*. While strategic alliances share to some extent the same characteristics as the above-mentioned transactions—that is, shared risk, shared rewards, shared management, etc.—the term "strategic alliances" is most often associated with Internet transactions, such as "cross-bannering" or "domain lease and development" agreements. In past years, international business transactions sought to increase productivity directly, but in recent years, strategic alliances seek to increase productivity indirectly, by nurturing formal and informal business relationships.[126] Nevertheless, the same complexities and challenges arise in both traditional

---

125. See JOINT VENTURES IN THE INTERNATIONAL ARENA (Darrell Prescott & Salli A. Swartz, eds. 2003), at pages 1–2. The following few paragraphs draw liberally from this source.

126. *Id.* at page 2.

international business transactions and innovative strategic alliances. These complexities and challenges can be summarized by considering the following questions:

- Which transaction should be used?—For example, the most common form of a joint venture is a corporation, but for tax reasons, it might be more prudent to form a branch or subsidiary, a partnership, a limited liability company, or some local variation thereof.
- Who should be included in the transaction?—One of the most important keys to success of any international business transaction is the choice of a business partner. Failure of business transactions may occur for many uncontrollable reasons, such as changing market conditions or unforeseeable natural catastrophes, but the choice of a trustworthy and credible business partner is essential for success.
- What form of financing should be used?—This question involves several aspects, such as how much financing will be required, and who shall provide it. For instance, financing for a joint venture may come solely from the parties involved, in the form of equity, or it may come from an outside source, in the form of a loan.
- How long will the strategic alliance endure, if one exists?—A strategic alliance between businesses may be established for only one specific transaction, or it may be used to nurture a series of transactions. For example, when forming a joint venture, "exit strategies" need to be negotiated. This will involve finding answers to questions on the term of the joint venture, transfers of joint venture interests, and restrictions on transfers of interests.[127]

The following sections in this chapter will discuss in more detail some of these (and other) complexities and challenges in international business transactions. Sections B and C of this Chapter deal with sales of goods across borders, first explaining some rules gov-

---

127. *Id.* at pages 3, 4, 6, and 13.

erning the transactional aspects of such sales and then explaining some rules bearing on a country's ability to regulate the terms of such sales and the movement of imports and exports of particular goods into and out of its own national territory. Section D deals briefly with licensing and more fully with foreign direct investment. Because all of these types of international business transactions—sale of goods across borders, licensing of production abroad, and foreign direct investment—are increasingly becoming the subject of multilateral rules (that is, outside the jurisdiction of any one particular nation-state), Section E examines some of the most important international economic organizations that have been established to implement those multilateral rules, especially the World Trade Organization.

Further Readings on International Business Transactions in General

(in addition to the sources cited in footnotes in this section)

Global Business Law: Principles and Practice of International Commerce and Investment (Second Edition, 2006), by John W. Head

Letterman's Guide to International Business (1996), by G. Gregory Letterman

International Trade for the Nonspecialist (1997 Edition), edited by Paul H. Vishny

Guide to International Commerce Law (1998 Edition), by Paul H. Vishny

Agency and Distribution Agreements: An International Survey (1997 Edition), by Agustin Jausàs

Bank Guarantees in International Trade (Second Edition, 1996), by Roeland F. Bertrams

International Trade and Investment (Seventh Edition, 1993), by Franklin R. Root

Legal Aspects of Doing Business in Europe (International Business Series, 1996), edited by Dennis Campbell and Christian T. Campbell

Legal Aspects of Doing Business in North America (1997), by the same authors

Hornbook on International Business Transactions (2001), by Ralph H. Folsom, Michael Wallace Gordon, and John A. Spanogle

Legal Guide to International Business Transactions (1991), by Philip Raworth

Export Trade: Law and Practice of International Trade (Tenth Edition, 1993), by Clive M. Schmitthoff

Introduction to Transnational Legal Transactions (1995), edited by Marylin J. Risk and Roberta I. Shaffer

International Business Law (1993 Edition and 2000 Edition), by Ray August

Foreign Commerce and Investment in Market Economy Countries, by Hugo J. Hahn and Ludwig Gramlich, in International Encyclopaedia of Comparative Law, vol. XVII, chap. 22 (1989)

IV.B. International Sales of Goods— Transactional Aspects

A sale of goods across national borders involves many **special features** that are not present when goods are sold within a country (that is, a domestic sale, without crossing any national borders). Several of those special features result in increased risk to both a buyer and a seller. For example, a sale of goods across national borders naturally involves two legal systems (or perhaps even more). In many cases, a sale of goods across borders will also involve two languages—not just spoken languages but "business languages" as well.

Assume, for example, that Bubba, the hypothetical US company referred to in section A of this Chapter, decides to sell its Bubcar automobiles to a company in the Netherlands that offers to pay a good price for the automobiles. What law will apply to that contract—US law or Dutch law or some other kind of law? Will the Dutch buyer have the same assumptions and expectations about which of the two parties is to be responsible for shipping the goods from the USA to the Netherlands, or for insuring the goods during that shipment? If Bubba ships the automobiles to the Netherlands and then the Dutch company refuses to pay for them, what remedy will Bubba have? In what courts can Bubba make a complaint against the Dutch company?

As these questions suggest, *an international sale of goods raises important issues and risks.* Fortunately, the international community has devised fairly effective methods of dealing with those issues and risks. For one thing, a special "language" of terms has been widely adopted in order to establish clearly and in detail how the costs and responsibilities of the parties to an international sales transaction are to be allocated among those parties. In addition, a set of multilateral rules (that is, applicable over most of the world, not specific to any one country) has been widely adopted to govern international sales transactions. The following subsections explain the special "language" and rules that have been established.

IV.B.1. Commercial Terms—FOB & CIF

Over several centuries, individual national legal systems have developed their own specific definitions of commercial terms. These include "Free on Board" (often called FOB for short) and "CIF" (originally referring to "cost, insurance, and freight"). The purpose of these terms was to identify, without having to state in detail in a sales contract, which of the parties was responsible for paying for the shipment of goods, when the title to the goods would pass from the seller to the buyer, which party (if either) was responsible for purchasing insurance to cover any loss or damage to the goods while they were passing from the seller to the buyer, and so forth.

For the most part, each country had its own set of commercial terms. In fact, within any one country's legal system, there might be more than one form of FOB or CIF, and in many cases other terms also were used.

This *lack of uniformity* between national "business languages" naturally caused difficulties. Sellers and buyers in an international sales contract (that is, from different countries) would have to specify in great detail all the allocation of costs and responsibilities in a sales contract, or one or both of them would have to be very knowledgeable about the commercial terms in the other's country. Otherwise they would run the risk of having a sales transaction go off track because of a misunderstanding over which party was responsible for what part of the transaction.

In order to overcome this difficulty, and to bring some uniformity in "business language", a separate, *multilateral set of commercial terms* was created. In fact, several efforts in this respect were undertaken during the twentieth century. The dominant set of international commercial terms now in use by many countries is called "INCOTERMS", short for "international commercial terms". It was created largely by the International Chamber of Commerce ("ICC"). The most recent version of INCOTERMS was adopted in 2000.[128]

The two most widely used INCOTERMS are FOB (Incoterms) and CIF (Incoterms). In drafting international contracts, many traders will provide that the goods are being sold "FOB (Incoterms 2000)" or "CIF (Incoterms 2000)". Under *FOB* (Incoterms 2000), the seller is only responsible for delivering the goods to the port of shipment and (in the case of an ocean shipment) placing them on board the vessel. The buyer is responsible for all costs and risks beyond that point. Under *CIF* (Incoterms 2000), the buyer is responsible for delivering the goods all the way to the port of destination, and for insuring the goods during the ocean shipment.

Using the example raised above, assume that Bubba entered into a contract with a Dutch company for the sale and purchase of Bubcar automobiles. If the contract specifies the term "FOB Seattle (Incoterms 2000)", Bubba will be responsible for manufacturing the automobiles and placing them on board the vessel that the Dutch company has arranged to sail from Seattle to the Netherlands. The Dutch company will be responsible for everything after that, and owes the purchase price to Bubba from that point. If, on the other hand, the contract specifies the term "CIF Rotterdam (Incoterms 2000)", Bubba will be responsible for manufacturing the automobiles,

---

128. For an explanation of the most recent version of INCOTERMS, see Jan Ramberg, *Guide to INCOTERMS 2000* (1999). The 2000 version of INCOTERMS varies only slightly from the next most recent version, issued in 1990. See also Jan Ramberg, *Guide to INCOTERMS 1990* (1991).

shipping them to Rotterdam, and paying the cost of insuring them against certain types of loss or damage during shipment.

IV.B.2. Choice of Law, Conflicts of Law, and the CISG

As noted above, an international sales transaction involves at least two legal systems. This can cause problems to the parties involved in an international sale. For example, if the buyer claims that the goods as delivered by the seller do not conform to the specifications given in the contract, which country's rules (those of the seller's country or those of the buyer's country) should the parties, or a court, use in determining whether that claim is legitimate or not—and, if it is, in determining what kind of remedy is available to the buyer?

For purposes of illustration, assume that the contract of sale between Bubba and the Dutch company referred to above provided for Bubba to sell to the Dutch company, under the term CIF (Incoterms 2000) the following items: "2,000 Bubcar automobiles, model X, for use in the Netherlands". If Bubba delivers 2,000 Bubcar automobiles, model Y, to Rotterdam, can the Dutch company refuse to accept the automobiles because they do not comply with the safety and environmental standards that automobiles are required to meet in order to be used in the Netherlands? In legal terms, do the automobiles conform to the specifications of the contract, or do they not conform?

Different legal systems have different commercial laws. Maybe under the Dutch commercial code the seller is responsible for providing goods that will be suitable for the use that the buyer intends for them, at least if the seller is aware of the buyer's intentions. Maybe the applicable US commercial code has no such requirement. How can the parties, or a court, know which of the two different rules to apply?

The *parties can usually choose which law should apply*. At the time a contract is drafted, the parties will often include a provision specifying that the law of a particular country will be used in determining rights and duties under the contract. This is commonly referred to as a "choice-of-law" provision. Most countries' legal systems now permit the parties to an international sales contract to name any country's legal system in the choice-of-law provision, although some countries require local law to be used in some cases.

It is worth noting that there might be several choice-of-law provisions in an international commercial contract. Such provisions might refer parties of a dispute to as many as four different national or nongovernmental systems or rules of law: (i) laws that recognize and enforce the agreement to arbitrate, (ii) laws relating to arbitration procedures, (iii) laws relating to the substantive issues in dispute, and (iv) laws that recognize and enforce the arbitral award. For example, in a dispute between a Chinese toy company that produces yo-yos and an Australian distributor who distributes the yo-yos to the USA, the arbitration clause in their contract may designate that US federal law will determine recognition and enforcement of the agreement to arbitrate and the arbitral award, Chinese procedural law will govern the proceedings, and Australian substantive law will govern the substance of the dispute.[129]

Careless parties sometimes fail to include a choice-of-law provision on any of these topics. In that case, it might be completely unclear what set of rules to use in determining the rights and responsibilities of the parties, especially if a dispute arises between them. Most legal systems have rules to help their own courts in choosing what legal system to use if the parties to a contract failed to do so themselves. These are sometimes called *rules of "private international law"* and sometimes called rules of "conflicts of law". Generally speaking, such rules advise a court to consider which country has the strongest connection to, or interest in, the contract at issue. Let us return, for example, to the commercial dispute referred to a few paragraphs earlier, involving Bubba and the Dutch buyer. If the contract did not include any choice-of-law provision, a Dutch court might try to determine which country—the USA or the Netherlands—had the closest connection to, or most interest in, the contract; then the court would apply the law of that country.

In other cases, parties recognize the need for a choice-of-law provision in their contract but cannot agree to specify either the buyer's

---

129. See Alan Redfern, *supra* note 47, at pages 1–2.

country or the seller's country in the choice-of-law provision. For example, the Dutch company might be unwilling to have its contract with Bubba governed by US law, and Bubba might be unwilling to have the contract governed by Dutch law. In such a case the parties might specify a third country's law (for example, the law of England) in the choice-of-law provision.

As this discussion shows, several difficulties can flow from the fact that different countries have different commercial laws. Recently, most of the major trading countries in the world took action to overcome most of these difficulties. In 1988 an international treaty came into effect that created a new, *multilateral set of commercial rules.* It is named the "UN Convention on Contracts for the International Sale of Goods".[130] It is also called the "CISG" or the "Vienna Sales Convention".

The CISG reflects the views of many international experts on commercial law and draws from the experience of many different legal systems. In general, if a country accepts the treaty obligations that the CISG imposes—about 70 countries had done so as of mid 2007, and they account for about three-quarters of all world trade—then it agrees to apply the commercial rules set forth in the CISG.

More specifically, the CISG applies whenever the parties to a contract for the sale of goods have their principal places of business in two different countries (if both of those countries have accepted the CISG), unless the parties "opt out" of the CISG rules by specifying another legal system in a clear choice-of-law provision of the contract. As the CISG becomes more widely accepted and understood, more and more international sales contracts are governed by it. As one legal scholar has asserted, the CISG is one more tool operating in the international arena to overcome the problem of "nationality of law". That is, as CISG jurisprudence grows, its application becomes more uniform across national boundaries, which in turn promotes international trade and sales.[131]

---

130. The CISG is cited at note 42, *supra.* For a list of CISG Contracting States, see http://cisgw3.law.pace.edu.

131. See Larry A DiMatteo et al., International Sales Law: A Critical Analysis of CISG Jurisprudence (2005), at page 163.

The CISG includes detailed rules on contract formation (that is, what circumstances have to occur before a contract is considered final), contract interpretation (how to construe the words of a contract if they are vague or inconsistent with each other), responsibilities of the seller (to deliver conforming goods in a timely manner and at the proper place), responsibilities of the buyer (to accept the goods and pay for them), and remedies of either party in case of a breach of contract by the other. In promulgating these rules, the CISG also operates on certain principles, some general or specific, others express or implied. These principles include the principle of favoring the continuation of a contract, the principle of good faith in international trade, and others.[132]

IV.B.3. Choice of Forum and Means of Dispute Resolution

The preceding subsection discusses choice of law—that is, which substantive rules will govern an international sales contract. A related question concerns *choice of forum*. Many international sales contracts specify not only (a) which substantive rules will govern the interpretation and application of the contract but also (b) which court system should have jurisdiction over a dispute if the parties cannot resolve it themselves.

For example, the hypothetical sales contract referred to above between Bubba and the Dutch company for the sale of automobiles might provide that "any dispute arising from this contract that the parties cannot resolve by mutual agreement will be submitted to the courts of the USA." This is a choice-of-forum clause.

It is important to include such a clause in an international sales contract because it will establish in writing what the parties intended regarding the "forum" in which any disputes should be raised. Usually, courts will honor those clearly stated intentions. For example, if a sales contract included the choice-of-forum

---

132. *Id.* at pages 23–27.

clause quoted in the preceding paragraph, a Dutch court would usually decline to accept a complaint later raised by the Dutch company about whether the Bubcar automobiles met the specifications required in the contract.

As noted in section B of Chapter II of this book, litigation in court is not the only way to settle legal disputes. In fact, in international sales transactions, litigation is very often considered to be inferior to another form of dispute resolution—arbitration.

International commercial arbitration has become increasingly popular and sophisticated in the past two or three decades. There are several reasons for this. Usually, commercial arbitration is considered to have the following advantages over court litigation:

- arbitration is faster than litigation;
- arbitration is less formal and less procedurally complicated than litigation;
- the persons who serve as arbitrators can be chosen by the parties, so they are much more likely to be knowledgeable about commercial and technical matters than court judges;
- the fact that the arbitrators (and the procedural rules under which they operate) can be chosen by the parties also increases the likelihood that the arbitral proceedings will be considered fair by both parties, particularly because the arbitrators are not part of either party's formal judicial system;
- likewise, in arbitration, the language of proceedings, the substantive law to be applied, and the place of arbitration can all be chosen by the parties;
- arbitration, unlike litigation, can be carried out privately, without publicity and exposure of confidential information; and
- arbitral awards (the results of arbitration) can be enforced in the courts of many countries—usually more easily than the judgments of national courts can be enforced.

Several of these perceived advantages apply to any arbitration, whether used in domestic disputes or in international disputes. (See, for example, section B of Chapter II, above.) Some, however, apply only (or with more vigor) to international disputes.

The last of the items enumerated above, regarding *enforcement of arbitral awards*, warrants special attention. The 1958 New York Convention[133] provides that the courts of any country that has adopted that treaty must recognize and enforce an arbitral award made in any other country that also has adopted the treaty, unless it would be inconsistent with important public policy considerations or unless certain other narrowly-defined exceptions apply. Most major trading countries (over 130 in all), have adopted the New York Convention. Hence, arbitral awards can usually be enforced in other countries. This encourages the use of arbitration as a means of dispute settlement in international sales.

For example, if Bubba and the Dutch company referred to in the hypothetical case above cannot resolve amicably a dispute that arises between them, they might refer the dispute to arbitration. Procedurally, this could happen in either of two ways. First, the parties might have specified in their contract that disputes are to be settled by arbitration. Alternatively, the parties might not have done that but might decide, once a specific dispute arises, to enter into a separate arbitration agreement that submits the dispute to an arbitral tribunal.

International commercial arbitration has been aided by the establishment of several sets of rules and several institutions that actually carry out the arbitration or provide experts to serve as arbitrators. One common set of rules is the UNCITRAL Arbitration Rules.[134] The UNCITRAL is a commission associated with the UN and is responsible for developing international trade law. In addition, the International Chamber of Commerce ("ICC") has its own set of rules and is available to provide arbitration services to international businesses.

---

133. United Nations Convention on the Recognition and Enforcement of Foreign Arbitral Awards, done at New York, June 10, 1958, entered into force June 7, 1959, reprinted in 330 UNITED NATIONS TREATIES SERIES at page 38. For information about parties to the Convention, see the UNCITRAL website, at www.unictral.org.

134. See Report of the United Nations Commission on International Trade Law on the Work of Its Ninth Session, reprinted in 15 INTERNATIONAL LEGAL MATERIALS (1976), at page 701. See also the UNCITRAL website, at www.uncitral.org.

Another important institution in the area of international arbitration, the International Centre for the Settlement of Investment Disputes ("ICSID"), deals mainly with disputes over investments, as distinct from those arising out of the sale of goods, and is therefore discussed in section D of this Chapter.

IV.B.4. Payment Provisions

The preceding subsections discuss various special difficulties or risks that arise in international sales contracts. Another risk—in fact a pair of risks—must be considered. In a sale of goods across borders, the buyer and seller are in different countries, often with considerable distance between them and therefore considerable cost in getting goods from the seller to the buyer. In addition, most such sales are large in quantity and value. Moreover, the distance involved, and the differences in language and culture, will often make it more difficult to judge with confidence the creditworthiness of the other party to the transaction or to exert influence over that other party in case a transaction goes off track.

In those circumstances, a seller of goods would usually prefer to be paid for the goods before shipping them to the buyer. If the seller were to ship the goods to the buyer before receiving payment, the seller runs a large financial risk. For example, if Bubba were to ship 2,000 automobiles to the Dutch company, in the hypothetical example given above, and then the Dutch company were for some reason to refuse to accept and pay for the automobiles when they arrive in Rotterdam, what can Bubba do? As discussed above, a well-drafted international sales contract will provide for a choice of law and a choice of forum; but during the time it takes to take action through litigation or arbitration, Bubba will not have been paid. Moreover, if Bubba were to lose a case conducted through such litigation or arbitration, Bubba might have to retrieve the 2,000 automobiles from Rotterdam or sell them there at a huge loss. Indeed, even if Bubba were to win the case but it turned out that the Dutch company is bankrupt and cannot pay the purchase price, Bubba would likewise have to retrieve or sell the automobiles at a loss. In short, the seller wants payment in advance.

The buyer, by contrast, would prefer to delay payment until after the buyer has actually received and inspected the goods, or at least until after the buyer has received proof that the goods have been shipped to the buyer and that they meet the specifications required under the contract. Otherwise, the buyer might find itself in a situation of having already paid for goods that were not received (or maybe not even shipped), or of receiving goods that do not meet the specifications required under the contract.

These apparently conflicting preferences of the seller and the buyer regarding payment can be largely overcome by *special payment arrangements* that have been developed in international law and practice. These arrangements concentrate around a letter of credit.

Specifically, the seller and buyer in an international commercial transaction can minimize the risks described above by constructing what is often referred to as a *"documentary international sale-of-goods transaction, using a negotiable bill of lading, with payment by irrevocable confirmed letter of credit"*. In such a transaction, banks serve as intermediaries between the two parties, facilitating the payment of the purchase price. What is sold and bought in a documentary sale is, in fact, documents. One of those documents, the bill of lading, represents title in the goods. When a seller ships the goods, the seller receives from the carrier (the company operating the vessel) a negotiable bill of lading stating that the seller placed the goods on board the vessel, apparently in good condition, and paid the cost of transporting the goods to the port of destination named by the buyer. Upon receiving that negotiable bill of lading, the seller presents it and several other required documents to a bank in the seller's home country. Under a commitment that that bank (the "confirming bank") made at the request of another bank in the buyer's home country (the "issuing bank"), the confirming bank immediately pays the seller the amount of the purchase price. The documents and payment are routed through the issuing bank to the buyer, who surrenders the negotiable bill of lading to the carrier in return for receiving the goods at the port of destination. Rules governing the use of letters of credits in international sales transactions are set forth in the Uniform Customs and Practice ("UCP") prepared and updated regularly by the International Chamber of Commerce ("ICC").

The confirmed letter of credit transaction described above (in simplified form) greatly reduces—indeed, almost eliminates—the seller's risk of non-payment. At the same time, it greatly reduces the buyer's risk of having paid and then receiving no goods or non-conforming goods.

Further Readings on Transactional Aspects of the International Sales of Goods

(in addition to the sources cited in footnotes in this section)

See the items listed at the conclusion of section A of this Chapter, especially *Global Business Law*, by John W. Head.

International Contracts and Payments (1991), edited by Petar Sarcevic and Paul Volken

International Encyclopedia of Laws: Commercial and Economic Law, edited by Jules H.V. Stuyck

Dictionary of International Trade (1994), by Edward G. Hinkleman

International Sales Law: A Critical Analysis of CISG Jurisprudence (2005), by Larry A. DiMatteo et al.

Guide to INCOTERMS 2000 (1999), by Jan Ramberg

International Case Law and Bibliography on the UN Convention on Contracts for the International Sale of Goods (1996 Edition), by Michael Joachim Bonell

Understanding the CISG in the USA (Second Edition, 2004), by Joseph Lookofsky

Law and Practice of International Commercial Arbtitration (Fourth Edition, 2004), by Alan Redfern and Martin Hunter

Enforcement of Foreign Judgments (1995 Edition), edited by Louis Garb and Julian Lew

International Litigation and Arbitration (2006), by Russell J. Weintraub

International Litigation: A Guide to Jurisdiction, Practice and Strategy (Third Edition, 1998), by David Epstein, Jeffrey L. Snyder, and Charles S. Baldwin

IV.C. International Sales of Goods— Regulatory Aspects

The preceding section of this Chapter focuses on several important transactional aspects of a sale of goods across national borders. The legal points discussed there should be borne in mind in the preparation of contracts for such sales. However, there is also another set of considerations that apply not to the private business relationship between a seller and a buyer but instead to the governmental regulation of imports and exports.

IV.C.1. Government Regulation of Imports— Tariffs and Other Barriers

A tariff is a tax on the importation of an article into a country. Traditionally, individual *countries have used tariffs for three main purposes*: (i) to provide revenues to the government; (ii) to protect domestic industries against competition from imported articles; and (iii) to carry out the foreign policy of the government—for example, by denying import privileges to countries with which the government has policy disputes. In some periods of history, tariffs between countries—that is, the level of import taxes charged on articles entering one country from another—have been very high. In the period between World War I and World War II, governments in the USA and many European countries imposed tariffs equal to 50% or even 100% of the value of the goods being imported.

Tariffs are not the only form of restriction on imports, of course. Other restrictions, often referred to as *"non-tariff barriers"*, include quotas (under which a government specifies a maximum amount of imports of a particular article from a particular country) or outright bans (prohibitions) on imports of specified articles.

From the perspective of a consumer, of course, these forms of re-striction on imports are generally disfavored because they have the effect of raising the prices of goods that consumers want. Neverthe-less, import restrictions have been widely used by governments, es-pecially for the purpose of protecting local industries that have in-fluence with those governments.

Within any particular country, the specific restrictions on im-ports usually take the form of legislation, or sometimes they take the form of regulations issued by a government agency acting on be-half of the executive or the parliament. A lawyer advising a client about the tariff to be paid on an article entering the country should refer to the "tariff schedules"—that is, the printed, publicly-avail-able list of tariffs.

Usually a *three-step procedure* must be followed in order to deter-mine the amount of a tariff on a particular article. First, the article itself must be identified for purposes of the tariff schedules. Some-times this step, which is often called "product classification", is diffi-cult to do because the descriptions in the tariff schedules might not match exactly the particular article being imported. Second, the country of origin of the article must be determined. Usually this is easy, but sometimes finished merchandise incorporates parts or ma-terials that have themselves come from several different countries.

Based on these first and second steps, the "tariff rate" can be de-termined. The tariff rate is usually expressed as a percentage of the value of the article. Therefore, as a third step, the value of the article must be determined. That value is multiplied by the tariff rate to de-termine the actual amount of tariff to be paid on the article.

IV.C.2. The GATT and the WTO

In the past 60 years, multilateral rules have been adopted that place limits and conditions on the ability of governments to impose import restrictions. Although these rules are, technically speaking, volun-tary—a country can adopt the rules or not, as it wishes—the rules are in fact almost universally accepted. Therefore they apply to nearly all international sales transactions.

The most important of these multilateral rules appear in a 1947 treaty, the General Agreement on Tariffs and Trade ("*GATT*"), as amended from time to time since then.[135] The GATT establishes four main principles:

(1) the principle of "*most favored nation*" ("MFN") treatment. This means that a country that is a party to the GATT is obligated to provide the lowest tariff rates (on any particular article) to other GATT countries. Put differently, this means that GATT Country X must not charge a tariff (duty) on an article from another GATT country at a rate any higher than the tariff rate Country X applies to that same type of article when coming from Country X's "most favored" trading partners.

(2) the "*national treatment*" principle. This means that a GATT country cannot impose any discriminatory burdens on imported merchandise *after* the merchandise has entered the country. This principle disallows, for example, the imposition of a special sales tax that would apply to foreign-made (imported) merchandise but would not apply to domestically-made merchandise.

(3) the "*Anti-NTB*" principle, or the principle that a GATT country cannot maintain any non-tariff trade barriers ("NTBs"). Instead, all restrictions on imports must be put in the form of tariffs, which are "transparent"—that is, an importer can know in advance just what the cost will be of importing an article into that country.

(4) the principle of "*bound duty rates*". Each GATT country has agreed, on accepting the GATT obligations, to a specific set of maximum tariff rates, which it cannot exceed without specific justifications provided for in the GATT. Over time, these country-specific sets of "bound duty rates" have been negotiated downward, so that now the average tariff rates existing in

---

135. General Agreement on Tariffs and Trade, done Oct. 30, 1947, entered into force Jan. 1, 1948, reprinted in 55 UNITED NATIONS TREATY SERIES, at page 187.

the major industrialized countries is around 5%, compared with about 40% a half-century ago.

By accepting the GATT, a country agrees to follow these four principles. The four principles are subject to some important exceptions and conditions. For example, certain *developing countries are usually given special preferential tariff treatment* for articles exported from those countries into economically developed countries. That is, articles from those countries will be exempted from any (or most) tariff duties on being imported into an industrialized country such as the USA or a European country.

Another exception applies to "unfair" imports, the most important of which are imports that are "dumped" or subsidized. A "dumped" article is one that is sold in the country of importation at a price that is less than the price at which the same article is sold in the home country where it is produced. For example, if an automobile produced in Japan is sold in the USA for US$30,000, and the same style automobile is sold in Japan for the equivalent of US$35,000, the automobile sold in the USA is being "dumped". The significance of this is that upon a proper finding that an article is being "dumped" in a country, and that this is causing injury to the domestic industry in that country, that country may impose an additional tariff in an amount equal to the "dumping margin"—that is, the margin between the sale price in the home country and the sale price in the country of importation. In the example given above, the USA would be permitted to impose an additional tariff, an *antidumping duty* of US$5,000 on imports of the automobile from Japan.

A subsidized article is an article that benefits from a subsidy provided by a government in the country where the article is produced. A subsidy is a payment or other form of preferential financing (for example, loans made at below-market interest rates) given to a company. The GATT prohibits many kinds of such subsidies—for example, subsidies that are calculated on the basis of how many articles a company exports—and permits a country that such an article is being imported into to impose an additional tariff (again, if there is injury in the importing country). The amount of the additional tariff, called a *"countervailing duty"*, is equal to the amount of the subsidy from which the article benefits.

Since 1947, when the GATT was first adopted, the rules on "dumping" and subsidies—and in many related areas as well—have been extended and refined. These changes have usually taken place in the context of "rounds" of multilateral trade negotiations. The two most recent rounds of such trade negotiations were the Tokyo Round, completed in 1979, and the Uruguay Round, completed in 1993.

The *Uruguay Round* was the most significant of all the multilateral trade negotiations of the last 50 years. It resulted in the creation of a new international organization, the *World Trade Organization*, which is responsible for the implementation of a greatly expanded set of treaties governing international trade.[136] These treaties build upon the 1947 GATT, as it has been amended through the years, and establish rules governing such things as: the valuation of articles for customs purposes; the imposition of additional duties on "dumped" and subsidized articles; imposition of additional duties, or use of other forms of import restrictions, to guard against a flood of imports that would threaten a country's economic health; trade in agricultural commodities; trade in meat and dairy products; trade in aircraft; and procurement of goods by governments. In addition, the Uruguay Round treaties extended the old GATT regime to include services and investment as well (in part), so that some of the same principles of free trade that have governed trade in goods apply as well to other forms of international business.

Only a few years old, the WTO has already become a powerful organization, partly because a country must join it and agree to nearly all the other treaties emerging from the Uruguay Round in order to be guaranteed the benefits of most favored nation (MFN) treatment. Indeed, most countries in the world have become or are becoming members of the WTO. As a consequence, the rules governing how a country can regulate imports are becoming liberalized and harmonized all over the world. This is designed to increase even further the

---

136. See the Agreement Establishing the World Trade Organization, done Dec. 15, 1993, entered into force Jan 1, 1995, reprinted in 33 INTERNATIONAL LEGAL MATERIALS (1994), at page 13.

volume of international sales transactions—and it is quite likely to achieve that aim. Further efforts in this direction were taken under a new round of trade negotiations launched at a WTO meeting in Doha in late 2001. These *Doha Round* negotiations focused on the developing countries' demands for increased access to developed countries' markets for agricultural products, textiles, clothing, and footwear.[137] Because these demands and other grievances have not been sufficiently addressed or settled, at least to some extent, by any new multilateral compromises, the Doha Round negotiations have failed to gain momentum and faltered seriously in 2006.

IV.C.3. Government Regulation of Exports

Just as most governments regulate imports, most governments also regulate exports—although to a much lesser degree. Usually a country wants to increase the level of its exports because those exports bring foreign exchange into the country. At the same time, a country might have important *reasons for controlling exports*—that is, for restricting the flow of goods out of its territory. Three such important reasons are: (i) to protect *national security* (a country would not, for example, want to permit the export of military arms to one of its enemies); (ii) to serve other important *foreign policy* interests (a country might want to prohibit all trade with a country with which it is on unfriendly terms); and (iii) to guard against *short supply* (a country might want to limit or prohibit the export of rice if a serious rice shortage were predicted for the following year).

Export controls, unlike import controls, are not heavily regulated by multilateral agreements. During the Cold War, some of the industrialized countries participated in a *multilateral set of export controls* managed by CoCom, the Coordinating Committee on Multilateral Export Controls. CoCom no longer exists, but a successor regime—having a broader group of participating countries but less clear direction so far—has been formed to carry out some of the

---

137. See THE WTO AND THE DOHA ROUND: THE CHANGING FACE OF WORLD TRADE (Ross P. Buckley, ed., 2003), at page 2.

same purposes. (It is called the Wassenaar Arrangement.) For example, most countries have agreed among themselves to limit the exportation of certain types of military arms to countries that are considered risks to international peace and security.

Within any particular country, a set of licensing controls usually applies to all or most exports. That means that any company wanting to export goods from the country will need to determine what kind of license, if any, must be obtained from the government in order for the export transaction to proceed. In some cases the exporting company will be responsible for the end-use of the exported goods in the country to which the goods are exported.

Further Readings on Regulatory Aspects of the International Sales of Goods

(in addition to the sources cited in footnotes in this section)

See the items listed at the conclusion of section A of this Chapter.

Modern GATT Law (2008), by Raj Bhala

The GATT Negotiations: A Business Guide to the Results of the Uruguay Round (1994), by John Kraus

Regulation of International Trade (1999 Edition), by Michael J. Trebilcock and Robert Howse

International Trade and Investment in a Nutshell (2000 Edition), by Ralph H. Folsom, Michael Wallace Gordon, and John A. Spanogle

International Trade and Economic Relations (Third Edition, 2004), by Ralph H. Folsom, Michael Wallace Gordon, and John A. Spanogle

The Results of the Uruguay Round of Multilateral Trade Negotiations— The Legal Texts (1995), by World Trade Organization

The Uruguay Round and the Developing Countries (1996), edited by Will Martin and L. Alan Winters

Anti-Dumping under the WTO: A Comparative View (1996), by Keith Steele

Guide to GATT Law and Practice 1947–1994 (1995), by World Trade Organization

The WTO and the Doha Round (2003), edited by Ross P. Buckley

IV.D. International Licensing and Investment

As explained above, government regulation of international trade (especially imports of goods) has been subjected to multilateral rules, most significantly the GATT. The same is not generally true of the government regulation of international licensing and investment. Instead, most of the rules on that subject are purely national in scope and source. Accordingly, a lawyer advising a client on the establishment or operation of one of these other forms of international business transaction will need to examine closely the rules within the particular country where the transaction is to take place.

IV.D.1. Licensing and Investment in General

The differences between international sales, international licensing, and international investment were discussed briefly in section A of this Chapter. "*Licensing of production abroad*" is the term used to describe an arrangement in which a company from one country agrees to let a "licensee" in another country use the company's design, production techniques, name, and maybe trademark in producing and selling goods in the licensee's country—or, in some cases, in third countries. Such arrangements will always be subject to government regulation in the licensee's country. For example, such a licensing arrangement might require government approval in order to be established; the licensing contract might need to comply with certain legal requirements of the licensee's country; and the payment of fees and royalties by the licensee to the licensing company might be subject to exchange controls. The list of possible restrictions is long, and advice from lawyers in the licensee's country will almost always be necessary.

Foreign direct investment is the third main form of international business transactions. The term "foreign direct investment", for these purposes, refers to the establishment or operation of a business entity in a "host" country with the involvement (sometimes minor, sometimes exclusive) of persons who are not nationals of the host country but instead come from a foreign country (the "home" country). Foreign direct investment should not be confused with a *portfolio investment*, where an individual or other entity may purchase shares in a company formed or functioning in another country, but where that purchase buys no connection to the management and control of the foreign company.[138]

There are several common risks that need to be considered and for which businesses must be prepared when engaging in foreign direct investment transactions:

- Political hostility—this often originates in the "host" country from some form of ideological opposition to foreign investment. It can also originate from a sense of nationalism, where the "host" country may fear foreign domination of its economy and therefore implement certain rules, regulations, and other restrictions concerning foreign investment. Foreign investors must be wary of the political risks of new or existing governments that may renegotiate contracts or expropriate tangible or intangible assets and other business property without fair compensation. Foreign investors must also be wary of deterioration in the general law and order of the "host" country or development of political corruption that may pose a risk to their foreign investments and transactions.
- Changes within an industry—due to economic industry developments that occur internationally, nationally within the "host" country, or nationally within the "home" country, foreign investors may need to renegotiate and reorganize their transactions in the "host" country.

As is the case with licensing, discussed above, most rules limiting or governing foreign investment appear at the national level—or sometimes at the bilateral level (that is, in agreements between two states)—rather than at the multilateral level. Although multilateral regulation is the exception rather than the norm in this area, two im-

---

138. See M. Sornarajah, THE INTERNATIONAL LAW ON FOREIGN INVESTMENT (2d ed. 2004), at page 7. The following paragraph also draws from this source, at page 77.

portant developments of recent years are relevant to any discussion regarding the law governing foreign direct investment. These developments, discussed in the next three paragraphs, are (i) general trends making national rules on foreign investment increasingly similar, and (ii) new attempts dating from the early the 1990s to make national rules on foreign investment conform to certain minimal international standards.

First, some *general trends* are apparent among most countries, especially less economically developed countries. In the 1970s, many such countries imposed intense restrictions on the entry of foreign investors into their economies. For example, it was illegal for a foreign investor to own more than 49% of the shares of a company in Mexico—or even 30% in some sectors of the economy—in the 1970s, without special exemption being granted by the government. Such restrictions, in Mexico and elsewhere, were designed to reduce foreign influence in the "host" country and to promote national economic self-sufficiency.

By the 1990s, the situation had changed dramatically, for two main reasons: (i) the debt crisis that put the economies of many developing countries in jeopardy in the early 1980s forced many of them to lower their barriers to foreign investment; and (ii) the fall of the Soviet Union in the 1990s, and the corresponding move away from central economic planning and toward market-based economies, further liberalized investment rules. This trend toward investment liberalization gained additional momentum as a result of the Asian financial crisis of 1997.[139]

Second, an important feature of the set of agreements emerging from the Uruguay Round of trade negotiations, concluded in the early 1990s, is the so-called "*TRIMs Agreement*" relating to "trade-related investment measures". Under this agreement, which every member of the World Trade Organization (successor to and enforcer of the GATT) is required to honor, a state must refrain from discriminating against foreign investors in many respects. Although important ex-

---

139. For a discussion of the Asian financial crisis, including the commitments toward investment liberalization that were sought as a condition to financial assistance by the International Monetary Fund and other lenders, see John W. Head, *Lessons from the Asian Financial Crisis: The Role of the IMF and the United States*, 7 KANSAS JOURNAL OF LAW AND PUBLIC POLICY (1998), at pages 70, 74.

ceptions apply, this general rule represents a step toward subjecting international investment to multilateral rules.

Further efforts to write multilateral rules for international investment were called for as part of the new Doha Round of trade negotiations, referred to above. It seems likely that such rules, if adopted, would resemble proposals made in the latter part of the 1990s as part of an unsuccessful attempt to create a *Multilateral Agreement on Investment*. That agreement would have provided broad protections to foreign direct investment assets and operations.

A final point regarding the development of multilateral standards governing international investment takes us back to the subject of *dispute resolution*, discussed in earlier sections of this book. For several decades the International Centre for the Settlement of Investment Disputes ("ICSID") has provided a forum in which private parties can bring legal complaints against national governments in respect of investments (as distinct from commercial transactions) that those private parties have in the countries ruled by those governments. The work of ICSID, which is a part of the World Bank Group and is headquartered in Washington, D.C., has given confidence to investors in establishing businesses outside their own countries and thereby has facilitated economic development—not only because it provides a forum that is regarded as neutral, competent, and fair, but also because it contributes to the overall development of multilateral standards governing international investment. Another institution associated with the World Bank Group—the Multilateral Investment Guarantee Agency ("MIGA")—also encourages international investment by providing insurance against various types of risk that such investment faces. Both ICSID and MIGA were established by treaties that most World Bank member countries have adopted.

IV.D.2. Themes and Provisions of Investment Regulations

In most countries, foreign investment is both welcomed and regarded with suspicion. Perhaps both views of foreign investment are warranted. Foreign investment is welcomed because it can provide significant *benefits to a national economy*. For example, foreign investment can:

- create *jobs* for the citizens of the host country, so that they can improve their incomes and their standards of living.
- create *investment opportunities* for the citizens of the host country, so that they can share in the earnings of new enterprises.
- increase the level of *exports* from the host country, bringing additional external income which can be used for various purposes to the benefit of the citizens.
- result in the *transfer of technical training* and know-how, which citizens can use in developing other enterprises and industries.
- broaden the potential for *self-sufficiency* of the host country by producing goods locally in substitution of imported goods.
- yield additional *tax revenues* which can be used for various purposes, to the benefit of the citizens of the host country.
- put the resources of the host country—both natural and human resources—to a better and *more productive use than before.*

On the other hand, experience in many countries has shown that *foreign investment warrants close scrutiny*, in order to guard against certain types of behavior—for example, environmental damage to precious natural resources, or an inappropriate introduction of different cultural values—that would run counter to the national interests of the host country.

For reasons mentioned above, many countries in recent years have revised their rules regarding foreign investment. These rules for the most part appear in special foreign investment laws or codes. In striking a *balance between liberalization and protection*, many countries have included in those laws or codes various combinations of the following approaches:

- regulating the *entry* of foreign investors by establishing a set of "negative lists", "restricted lists", and "promotion lists"—designating, respectively, those types of foreign investment (often classified by economic sector) that are (i) prohibited within the host country (either because they are reserved to the state itself or to citizens of the host country), (ii) permitted within the host country subject to the meeting of specified criteria, and (iii) promoted by the host country, sometimes with actual financial incentives being offered by the government. For example, an investment code might provide that the manufacture of military armaments or the operation of inter-island transport is off-limits to foreign investors, that the exploration drilling of oil on the continental shelf is open to foreign investors only up to a certain percentage of ownership, and that foreign investors are welcome in all other economic sectors without meeting any specific requirements.

- relying on existing laws, instead of the foreign investment law, as the principal means of regulating the *operation* of foreign investors. In other words, the trend is away from entrusting the supervision of foreign-owned business entities to government officials working on foreign investment matters. Instead, once a foreign investor or investment has been established in the host country, the existing rules and procedures for enforcement should apply. Hence, environmental rules, health-and-safety rules, anti-fraud rules, banking regulations, and anti-monopoly rules would be the mainstays of regulating foreign as well as domestic businesses and individuals.

- authorizing a *special agency* of the government to implement and enforce the rules relating specifically to foreign investment, and to fill in gaps where the legal system does not include adequate regulation in particular respects—for example, if other laws do not adequately provide for environmental protection.

- incorporating some basic *multinational rules or guidelines* on treatment of foreign investors. In addition to the non-discrimination standards of the TRIMs Agreement mentioned above, some foreign investment laws include provisions (i) limiting the circumstances in which nationalization or expropriation of investment property can take place and (ii) guaranteeing the free or easy repatriation of both profits and capital relating to the investment.

- offering *incentives* to investors or investments that are of special interest to the host country. These include, in addition to ordinary financial incentives (such as temporary tax relief), a number of other special regimes: establishment of special economic zones (in which foreign investors are allowed to operate under special rules designed to attract them to that area);

operation of free ports (facilities in port cities where importers can sort and store goods without taking them through customs offices); and creation of export processing zones (manufacturing facilities that are allowed to process foreign goods and materials for export without paying tariffs if the goods are re-exported).

In many countries, government regulation of foreign investment takes the form of *joint venture requirements*—that is, the requirement that foreign investors form joint ventures (discussed briefly at the beginning of this chapter) with local companies in order to carry on their desired economic activities. In some cases government regulations will dictate that the joint venture is not permitted to include more than a specified percentage (say, 30% or 50%) of foreign ownership or control—as in the Mexican regulations referred to above. In some countries the regulations will also include provisions that require, or at least, influence, certain other aspects of the structure and operation of a joint venture—such as

- the legal form of the business,
- the financing arrangements between the local partner and the foreign partner to the joint venture,
- how the joint venture will be governed,
- how intellectual property rights are to be handled within the business,
- arrangements for importation and exportation of items used by or produced by the business,
- what kinds of reports can be (or must be) submitted to the joint venture partners and to the government regulatory officials, and
- how the joint venture can be (or in some cases must be) concluded and wound up.

Although most countries have foreign investment regulations of the sort described generally above, it is worth noting that in many cases those national government regulations have been modified by *bilateral investment treaties.* Under such treaties—which in most instances run between an economically developed (capital-exporting) country and an economically less developed (capital-importing) country—some or all of the details referred to above will be addressed. In addition, such treaties will often stipulate rules and procedures for expropriation of foreign investment assets, providing for example that if the host government seizes such assets, the foreign investor is owed compensation under a formula specified in the treaty. Such treaties often cover numerous other issues as well, including tax, reporting, and trade matters.

Further Readings on International Licensing and Investment

(in addition to the sources cited in footnotes in this section)

See the sources listed at the conclusion of section A of this Chapter, especially *Global Business Law*, by John W. Head.

A Guide to International Joint Ventures with Sample Clauses (1999 Edition), by Ronald Charles Wolf

Joint Ventures in the International Arena (2003), edited by Darrell Prewscott and Salli A. Swartz

Investment Laws of the World (1972 as updated to 1996), ICSID [International Centre for the Settlement of Investment Disputes]

The International Law on Foreign Investment (Second Edition, 2004), by M. Sornarajah

Transnational Joint Ventures (1989), edited by Peter B. Fitzpatrick

International Joint Ventures: A Practical Guide (1992), by John P. Karalis

IV.E. International Economic Organizations

A last topic to be discussed under the heading of "relations with other economies" concerns the role and status of international economic organizations. One of these, the WTO, is discussed briefly in section C of this Chapter. It is one of three key organizations that a lawyer should be aware of in order to have a basic understanding of economic law. The other two organizations are the International Monetary Fund and the World Bank. The European Union will also be mentioned briefly.

At the close of World War II, leading politicians and economists identified *three key problems* that needed to be addressed effectively in order to avoid world economic disarray—and indeed to avoid a third World War. For each of these three problems, they also envisioned an international economic organization.

First, these people believed that the *high tariff levels* and other restrictions to international commerce that had existed between World War I and World War II should be dramatically reduced in order to increase world trade and thereby improve standards of living in all countries. For this purpose, they envisioned an International Trade Organization ("ITO").

Second, these people believed that another set of impediments to world trade—namely, *restrictions in the convertibility of national currencies*, and fluctuations in relative values of those currencies— had to be removed. It should be made possible, they reasoned, for a seller in France to accept Indian rupees in payment for goods sold to India, and to have confidence that those rupees could be changed into French francs at an exchange rate that would not change significantly over time. In order to establish and enforce rules of this nature, the International Monetary Fund ("IMF") would be created.

Third, it would be necessary to *rebuild Europe* and other countries ravaged by World War II, and to help developing countries build their economies as well. For this purpose, the World Bank (technically, the International Bank for Reconstruction and Development) would be established.

The second and third of these organizations—the IMF and the World Bank—were established in 1944 (a year before the UN was established) as a result of a conference with representatives from about 45 countries. They gathered at Bretton Woods, New Hampshire, in the northeastern USA, to finalize the charters of those two international economic organizations,[140] which are therefore called the *Bretton Woods Institutions.*

---

140. See Articles of Agreement of the International Monetary Fund, done July 22, 1944, entered into force Dec. 27, 1945, reprinted in 2 UNITED NATIONS TREATY SERIES at page 39; Articles of Agreement of the International Bank for Reconstruction and Development, done July 22, 1944, entered into force Dec.

The third organization, the ITO, was not created as planned because of resistance from the USA. Instead, the GATT, discussed above in section C of this Chapter, was established. The creation of the WTO in 1995 completes, in many respects, the work started by politicians and economists in the 1940s, because the WTO has many of the features and purposes that the ITO was to have.

These three organizations (the IMF, the World Bank, and the WTO) wield great power. Two of them, the IMF and the World Bank, are dominated by the rich industrialized countries, especially the "Group of Seven" ("G-7") countries. These are the USA, Japan, Germany, the United Kingdom, France, Canada, and Italy. Voting rights in the IMF and the World Bank are tied to shares of ownership. For example, the USA owns about 17% of the shares of the IMF, and the G-7 members combined own roughly 40% of the shares in that institution. As a result of this *"weighted voting"* system, the IMF largely reflects the economic views (and, to some extent, the political views) of the G-7 countries.

The purposes of the World Bank and the IMF have *changed over time.* For the first 25 years following World War II, the IMF managed a system of fixed exchange rates—that is, a system in which the relative values of the currencies of IMF member countries were fairly stable, with significant changes in those values permitted only upon IMF approval. That system collapsed, however, in the 1970s. From the mid-1980s, with the rise of the debt crisis, the most visible role of the IMF has been to lend money to developing countries to assist in their balance of payments—that is, the balance between (i) what they need to pay other countries for imports and debt repayments and (ii) what they receive from other countries from export earnings.

In making those loans, the IMF usually imposes *"conditionality"*— requirements concerning the borrowing countries' economic and financial policies. The main stated purpose of this "conditionality" is to help the borrowing countries' economic health and therefore en-

---

27, 1945, reprinted in 2 UNITED NATIONS TREATY SERIES at page 134. Both charters have been amended. The most significant amendment was to the IMF charter in the late 1970s to reflect the collapse of the par value system of exchange rates.

sure the repayment of the loans, so the funds will be available to lend again to other countries in need. However, many critics accuse the IMF of imposing incorrect or overly harsh conditions on borrowing countries.

The *role of the World Bank* has also changed, although not as much as that of the IMF. The rebuilding of Europe was carried out with assistance from the Marshall Plan, managed by the USA, so the World Bank focused its efforts from the late 1940s on the developing countries. Like the IMF, the World Bank lends money to developing countries. Those loans, however, are for a different purpose: to finance development projects such as schools, hospitals, roads, irrigation systems, airports, dams, telecommunications systems, and similar projects. Some of those projects are criticized for their environmental and social impact.

The actual role and long-term importance of the *WTO* and the extensive set of rules emerging from the Uruguay Round are not yet clear. Unlike the IMF and the World Bank, the WTO is based on a more democratic form of decision-making. Voting is on the basis of one-country-one-vote, so the USA and other G-7 countries do not have special power as a formal matter. Informally, however, those countries may be expected to continue their influence. Another difference between the WTO and the two Bretton Woods Institutions is also important: the WTO does not lend money. It can, however, authorize member countries to impose trade sanctions against a member country that refuses to meet its obligations under the various Uruguay Round agreements, discussed above in section C of this Chapter.

Those are the principal international economic organizations— the IMF, the World Bank, and now the WTO. Another international organization, the *UN*, has some economic functions, mainly through the Economic and Social Council ("ECOSOC"), and through the United Nations Development Program ("UNDP").

Other important economic organizations exist at the regional level. Four *regional development banks* have been established: the Asian Development Bank, the Inter-American Development Bank, the African Development Bank, and the European Bank for Reconstruction and Development. These institutions, like the World Bank, lend money to developing countries for economic development projects.

The *European Union*, formerly the European Community (and, before that, a set of three European Communities focusing on (i) iron and steel, (ii) economics generally, and (iii) atomic energy), is the vehicle by which most European countries are moving today toward economic and monetary integration. A single customs union and economic trading community exists now within the borders of the EU, and a single European currency and central bank were created near the end of the 1990s. As a consequence of these developments, and following substantial expansions of EU membership in recent years, the EU now constitutes a single economic and monetary union of several hundred million people—and proposals for its continued expansion would further increase the extent of its coverage in terms of both population and territory. Significantly, the EU represents a concentration of economic and political power existing above the level of the individual nation-state on which the international legal system has been based for the past 350 years.

Further Readings on International Economic Organizations

(in addition to the sources cited in footnotes in this section)

See the items listed at the conclusion of section A of this Chapter.

The Future of the Global Economic Organizations: An Evaluation of Criticisms Leveled at the IMF, the Multilateral Development Banks, and the WTO, by John W. Head (2005)

International Economic Organizations in the International Legal Process (1995), by Sergei A. Voitovich

The Law of Money and Financial Services in The European Community (2000 Edition), by J.A. Usher

The Legal Aspect of Money (Fifth Edition, 1992), by F.A. Mann

International Monetary Collaboration (Second Edition, 1996), by Richard W. Edwards, Jr.

About the Author

John W. Head is a professor of international and comparative law at the University of Kansas. He holds an English law degree from Oxford University (1977) and a US law degree from the University of Virginia (1979). Before starting an academic career, he worked in the Washington, D.C. office of Cleary, Gottlieb, Steen & Hamilton (1980–1983), at the Asian Development Bank in Manila (1983–1988), and at the International Monetary Fund in Washington (1988–1990). Both his teaching and his published works concentrate on the areas of international business and finance, public international law, and comparative law, with a special focus on dynastic Chinese law. His principal books include *Global Business Law: Principles and Practice of International Commerce and Investment* (2006), *Global Economic Organizations: An Evaluation of Criticisms Leveled at the IMF, the Multilateral Development Banks, and the WTO* (2005), and *Law Codes in Dynastic China* (2005, with Yanping Wang). He has taught in Austria, China, Hong Kong, Jordan, Mexico, Mongolia, Turkey, and the United Kingdom and has undertaken special assignments in numerous locations for international financial institutions and development agencies. Mr. Head is married to Lucia Orth. He and his wife live in the quiet wooded countryside southwest of Lawrence, Kansas.

Index